DISEASES

2nd Revised Edition

Volume 5

Immune system to Multiple sclerosis

Bryan Bunch

EDITOR
SCIENTIFIC PUBLISHING

GROLIER
EDUCATIONAL

Editor: Bryan Bunch

Design and production: G & H SOHO, Inc.
Design: Gerry Burstein
Prepress: Kathie Kounouklos

Writers:

Barbara Branca
Bryan Bunch
Barbara A. Darga
Betsy Feist
Gene R. Hawes
Wendy B. Murphy
Karin L. Rhines
Jenny Tesar
Bruce Wetterau
Gray Williams

Editorial assistant:
Marianne Bunch

Copyediting and index:
Felice Levy

Creative assistance:
Pam Forde

Illustrators:

Photographs:
Karin L. Rhines

Icons:
Steve Virkus and Karen Presser

Medical Illustrations:
Jean Cassels
Leslie Dunlap
Pamela Johnson
Joel Snyder

Library of Congress Cataloging in Publication Data

Main entry under title:
Diseases
v. < >' cm
Includes bibliographical references and index.
Summary: Alphabetically arranged articles present medical information
on more than 500 diseases, discussing causes, symptoms, stages of the
disease, its likelihood of striking, treatments, prevention, and long-term effects.

Set ISBN: 0-7172-5688-X
1. Diseases—Encyclopedias, Juvenile. [1. Diseases—
Encyclopedias.] I. Grolier Educational Corporation
R130.5 D57 1996
616.003—dc20   96-27606
                                CIP
                                AC

Revised edition published 2003.
First published in the United States in 1997 by
Grolier Educational, Sherman Turnpike, Danbury, CT 06816

COPYRIGHT © 2003, 1997 by SCIENTIFIC PUBLISHING, INC.

A HUDSON GROUP BOOK

Set ISBN: 0-7172-5688-X

Volume ISBN: 0-7172-5693-6

Immune system

The immune system is a complex and effective defense against all manner of ills, with important roles played by the skin, thymus, spleen, lymph system, and bone marrow. But the main soldiers in the war against foreign invaders of the body are white blood cells and the chemicals that they produce.

The foundation of the immune system is the difference between self (the cells and proteins of a person) and nonself (the cells, proteins, and many other substances of everything else in the world). Often biologists call the nonself materials *foreign*.

Size and location: The immune system pervades the body. Its first outposts are the skin and the stomach lining, barriers to microorganisms. The nose, mouth, throat, and lungs all contain substances (such as mucus and saliva) and mechanisms (such as cilia, tiny waving projections that move to expel foreign substances from the lungs) that trap and eliminate microbes.

Much of the immune system is located in lymph and blood. Lymphatic tissue forms organs such as the thymus in the upper breast, the adenoids and tonsils in the head, and the spleen in the abdomen. Bone marrow in the heart of bones is also a part of the lymphatic immune system.

Most of the activity of the immune system comes from roving cells that have been trained by the thymus. These form a diverse group usually lumped together as white blood cells, or *leukocytes*.

- *Lymphocytes*, found in lymph in profusion as well as in blood, form about a quarter of the white blood cells. These include several types of *granulocytes* (GRAAN-yuh-loh-SIYTZ), *B cells*, and the cells made famous by their low count in AIDS, the several types of *T cells*. The lymphocytes fight bacteria, viruses, and parasites primarily with chemical warfare but also by direct combat. Some T cells directly attack invading or foreign cells, while others coordinate the work of other lymphocytes.
- Phagocytes engage foreign invaders and even some wastes from body processes by physically engulfing and dissolving

the intruders. The largest of these are the *macrophages* (MAAK-ruh-FAY-juhz), which appear almost like amebas in their ability to move and to consume and digest bacteria or other foreign cells.

■ *Mast* cells are involved in allergic reactions, producing histamine among other chemicals used to fight infection.

One place where these immune system cells are stored until needed is the spleen. Blood passes through the spleen, which has a concentration of lymphocytes to attack intruders. Immune system cells are also found throughout the lymphatic system, especially in the nodes and throughout the bloodstream. When there is a source of infection, such as a cut, a place where bacteria are proliferating (for example, a boil or an abscess), or an organ that has developed cancerous cell changes, the immune system cells flock to the region.

Role: The immune system guards against infection in part by its amazing ability to remember what it has encountered in the past. Lymphocytes first learn the difference between self and nonself. The B cells are famous for producing *antibodies*, mole-

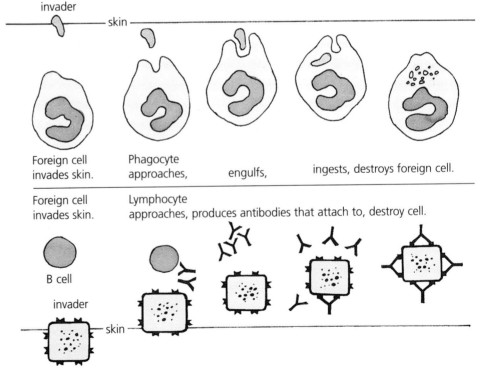

In the top row a white blood cell called a phagocyte destroys an invader by eating it. The B cell in the bottom row makes antibodies that attack the invader.

invader — skin

Foreign cell invades skin.

Phagocyte approaches,

engulfs,

ingests, destroys foreign cell.

Foreign cell invades skin.

Lymphocyte approaches, produces antibodies that attach to, destroy cell.

B cell

invader

skin

cules created to attack a specific foe. Antibodies are the agents of immunity whose production continues after the first exposure to a disease or after vaccination, enabling a quick and effective response to another attack by the same agent.

Conditions that affect the immune system: The immune system can err by reacting either too much or too little.

Allergic reactions: Often some part of the immune system reacts to a harmless substance in the environment as if the substance were a major enemy. Usually, the substance is some common food, such as eggs, or small particles, such as pollen or dust. These reactions are known as allergies. In some cases an immune overreaction can be fatal; the stimuli in such instances can be a bee sting or a medicine such as penicillin. Asthma, another potentially fatal immune reaction, involves spasms in the breathing apparatus.

A less common version of an allergy occurs when the immune system loses the distinction between self and nonself. In that case, instead of attacking harmless pollen or egg proteins, the immune system attacks some part of the body that it is supposed to defend. If the joints are attacked, for example, the result is rheumatoid arthritis. An attack on the insulin-producing cells of the pancreas produces the most dangerous form of diabetes mellitus. Sometimes many parts of the body come under fire, as in lupus.

Loss of immune function: An infection can overwhelm the immune system with great numbers of microorganisms or with some form of stealth, producing illness. In virtually every case, however, the immune system soon defeats the invader. People who succumb are often those with weak immune reactions—because they are very young, because they are very old, because they are poorly nourished, or because they are already ill with some other disease. Even a serious illness that can defeat a healthy immune system, such as tuberculosis or syphilis, is usually held in check for years.

But sometimes a genetic flaw produces a child with little or no immune response from birth. The flaw may be one of the group of immune failures known as SCID (severe combined immunodeficiency). Another genetic problem is known as ADA deficiency because the immune system is compromised by the lack of a chemical called ADA.

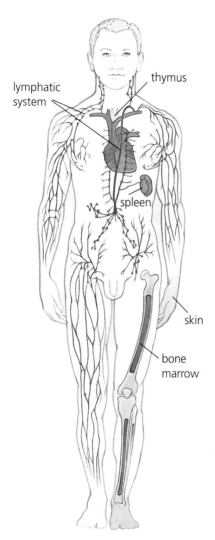

Much of the work of the immune system is carried out by the lymphatic system, thymus, and spleen, but bone marrow is the source of the white blood cells. The skin is not only the first line of defense; it also helps to train some white blood cells.

Both children and adults can be stricken with immune system collapse as a result of a virus that lives in and destroys certain classes of lymphocytes. The virus, known as HIV (human immunodeficiency virus), eventually reduces one population of T cells that is a key player in directing the immune response. As a result, the HIV-infected individual develops AIDS. With a seriously impaired immune system a person begins to lose the battles against common microorganisms. Germs that the immune system usually keeps in check suddenly begin to overwhelm the body. Although there are other symptoms of AIDS, the loss of immune function is usually the cause of death from an infection or from several all at once.

Turning off the system: In certain situations it is desirable to shut down the immune system, sometimes for life. A person suppresses a part of the system every time an antihistamine is used to lower an allergic response. Suppression of immune reactions is one way to treat an autoimmune disease.

The immune system recognizes a transplanted organ as nonself and sets out to destroy it. Organ transplants failed regularly until researchers located chemicals that suppress the immune system. These chemicals usually have to be taken for life by a person receiving a transplant to prevent rejection of the transplanted organ by the immune system.

Sometimes an even more devastating event occurs after a transplant; graft-versus-host reactions somehow turn the immune system around so that the transplant is accepted as self but the remainder of the body becomes nonself. In such a situation the immune system attacks the skin and sometimes the joints, heart, and other organs. The reaction, if it cannot be suppressed, is often fatal.

History: Although evidence of immune protection was known of in ancient times, the first inkling of how immunity is produced came in 1884, when the Russian-French bacteriologist Ilya Illich Mechnikov first observed macrophages at work. Immunologists, however, often date the discovery of the immune system to the discovery of antibodies by Emil von Behring and Shibasaburo Kitasato (independently) in 1890 and of blood types by Karl Landsteiner in 1900.

The immune system did not get real notice, however, until

There are many ways to strengthen the immune system, including both exercise and rest. Some fruits and vegetables, such as broccoli, contain chemicals known to improve immune function.

1983. That was the year that AIDS, the syndrome that has the loss of immune function as its main symptom, became widely recognized. It was also the year that physicians learned how to turn off parts of the immune system deliberately using the drug cyclosporine to stop immune system rejection of transplanted organs.

Impotence
(IHM-puh-tuhns)

SYMPTOM

See also
Cancers
Circulatory system
Diabetes mellitus, type II ("adult-onset")
Hypertension
Penis
Prostate gland
Reproductive system

Impotence, or *erectile dysfunction,* consists of inability to develop or continue an erection of the penis for a long enough time to carry out sexual intercourse.

Incidence: The risk of chronic erectile dysfunction typically increases with age. Some studies have indicated that among men who are 40 years old, complete erectile dysfunction is experienced by about 1 in every 20, while somewhat frequent dysfunction affects almost 1 in every 5. But among men age 70 some 3 in every 20 show complete dysfunction, while 1 out of every 2 exhibits somewhat frequent dysfunction. All in all, slightly more than half of men between the ages of 40 and 70 experience some impotence, and about 30 million men experience erectile dysfunction at a level that troubles them.

Cause: When a man is sexually stimulated (or at times during sleep with no stimulation), blood flows into channels in the penis, causing it to become stiff and elongated (erect). Impotence occurs when such blood flow fails to occur, often because the opening to the channels stay tightly or partially closed. Impotence is caused by some physical malfunction in eight out of every ten cases for adult men of all ages. In some cases the cause may be a low level of the male hormone testosterone (tehs-TOS-tuh-ROHN).

Associations: Circulatory system malfunctions, such as hypertension, seem to be the most frequent cause of impotence among men beyond their fifties. Diabetes mellitus may also produce problems in the circulatory system and consequently reduced blood flow for erection. In addition, it can impair the functioning of certain nerves essential to erection. Impairment of such nerves can also result from Parkinson's disease, multiple sclerosis, spinal cord injuries, or surgery to treat prostate cancer. Chronic or occasional heavy consumption of alcohol or street drugs frequently causes impotence, even among young men. Psychological causes of impotence can include severe depression, anxiety, stress, or exhaustion.

Treatment: In recent years the drug sildenafil (Viagra) has become the treatment of choice for many men, although it is not infallible. Viagra relaxes the parts of the circulatory system that permit blood to engorge the penis. For several hours after taking Viagra most men who have been sexually stimulated will develop an erection. Other drugs with similar action are being developed.

Physicians can provide one of three methods for producing erections in cases for which Viagra is ineffective. Medications can be injected into the penis for each erection wanted; permanent implants (partly rigid rods or inflatable tubes) can be inserted surgically in the penis; or suction devices can be employed to build up a vacuum around the penis, enabling it to become engorged with blood.

Incontinence

(ihn-KON-tuh-nuhns)

SYMPTOM

Incontinence consists of inability to control excretion of either urine or feces. In almost all cases adults subject to incontinence develop either the urinary type (*leaky bladder*) or the fecal (FEE-kuhl) type at any one time, rather than both.

Incidence: A few individuals continue bedwetting, that is, urinating unintentionally while asleep, after becoming toilet trained. Chronic bedwetting is termed *enuresis* (EHN-yuh-REE-sihs). About 13 million Americans experience urinary incontinence, with women twice as likely as men to have the condition. Many persons experience at least some degree of fecal incontinence as a result of diarrhea, with its almost irresistible, frequent urges to empty the bowels.

Both urinary and fecal incontinence are much more common in people over 65, with urinary incontinence affecting 1 out of 4 older people at least some of the time. Stroke is a common cause of this problem in older persons.

Parts affected: Muscles that close the anus or the opening of the urethra may fail or be weakened, causing incontinence. Causes of incontinence can also stem from other parts of the urinary or digestive tracts, or even other parts of the body. Both urinary and fecal incontinence often accompany alcoholism, especially when the person has been drinking heavily.

Associations: Pregnancy may cause pressure on the bladder that produces slight urinary leakage after physical effort. Bladder infections or stones may also produce urinary incontinence, as can enlargement of the prostate gland in elderly men. Loss of urinary control by the brain appears in some cases, such as in persons who have dementia.

Fecal incontinence frequently accompanies age-related muscle weakness and such diseases as diabetes, myasthenia gravis, or syphilis. Injury to the anal muscles or paralysis of the lower body can also result in fecal incontinence.

Relief of symptoms: Muscles weakened in childbirth or injury may be strengthened by special exercises directed at the anus and sphincter muscles that control urination. These are called Kegel exercises after Dr. Arnold Kegel, who originally developed them. Kegel exercises are useful in preventing or eliminating urinary incontinence in women who have had several pregnancies; they also are successful in controlling fecal incontinence in many older persons who have no underlying major problems.

Surgery or medication for urinary incontinence due to more severe injury or disease often resolves the problem. But if normal physical control cannot be restored, incontinence undergarments or devices can be used to enable a person to pursue almost all the activities of a normal life.

Fecal incontinence due to chronic constipation may be most

simply relieved by including large additional amounts of fiber in the diet. Treatment for fecal incontinence resulting from other causes can include enemas or laxative suppositories to empty the rectum at regular intervals, or surgery if indicated.

Indigestion	*See* **Gastritis; Heartburn; Nausea**
Infantile paralysis	*See* **Poliomyelitis ("polio")**

Infants and disease

REFERENCE

Infants are born with a certain amount of protection from disease that carries through the first year of life. This protection is passed from a mother to her child during pregnancy and then after birth through breast milk. Called *passive immunity,* this protection comes from the natural transmission of *antibodies,* chemicals that fight specific disease organisms. Passive immunity in infants helps prevent illnesses from occurring and shortens the course of a disease if it does occur.

Why infants respond to disease differently: Because of their small size infants have the added potential of experiencing serious complications from disease. For example, a common stomach "flu" (gastroenteritis) caused by a virus usually brings symptoms such as diarrhea or vomiting in both adults and infants. But in infants these symptoms can more easily lead to the potentially life-threatening problem of loss of bodily fluids, or dehydration.

Most serious diseases of infants are caused not by viruses

A newborn baby begins life with passive immunity derived from antibodies that its mother has acquired during her lifetime. *(Photo by Stephen McCarthy)*

but by *bacteria*. A bacterial infection is usually treated with a medication known as an *antibiotic*. Frequently, a physician will prescribe an antibiotic for an infant if a bacterial infection is merely suspected. The reason is that bacteria grow and spread rapidly in an infant's body. The earlier the medication is started, the more effective it is in killing the bacteria. Saving time and discomfort while waiting for laboratory test results is a good reason for starting treatment before diagnosis is confirmed. Antibiotics are not effective for viral diseases, however.

How a physician determines cause of disease: When an infant is showing disease symptoms, he or she may be brought to a specialist in children's diseases, a *pediatrician,* who will perform an examination. When infection is suspected, the physician may take blood and urine samples, x-rays, and a swab to culture from the location suspected to include disease-causing microorganisms. The swab lifts a sample of body tissues, which is then placed on a material that promotes growth of bacteria. For example, for a sore throat the swab would be taken from the back of the mouth and cultured. Laboratory technicians can determine types of bacteria from patterns of growth or microscopic examination of the culture.

If a hereditary disease is suspected, that is, one that has been inherited from parents, a family history of disease is usually discussed.

Types and treatments of infant diseases: Also see the entries on individual diseases or disease types.

Infectious disease: Infections are caused by microscopic organisms that invade an infant's body. When the body's immune system recognizes these foreign bodies, it begins to fight against the invasion by producing an army of immune cells called antibodies. Antibodies are chemicals produced by a kind of white blood cell. As blood rushes to the scene of the infection, it causes the site to look red. This immune response also increases the infant's body heat, causing a higher body temperature, or fever. As the antibodies destroy the microorganisms, the infection is reduced and eventually healed.

Bacteria can enter an infant's body in a variety of ways: by droplets released by a sneeze or cough that are breathed into the respiratory system; by ingestion into the digestive system; by

Types of infant diseases and causes

Infectious diseases

Bacterial infections	*Viral infections*	*Fungal infections*
Conjunctivitis (also viral)	Chicken pox	Candidiasis
Diphtheria	Conjunctivitis (also bacterial)	Pneumonia (also bacterial or viral)
Otitis media (also viral)	Croup	
Pertussis	Measles (rubeola)	
Pneumonia	Mumps	
(also viral or fungal)	Otitis media (also bacterial)	
Scarlet fever	Pneumonia (also bacterial or fungal)	
Staph infection	Rubella ("German" measles)	
Tonsillitis	Smallpox (no longer exists in the wild)	

Diseases with other causes

Congenital diseases (genetic or developmental)	*Environmental diseases*	*Parasitic diseases*	*Idiopathic diseases (of unknown cause)*
Autism	Fetal alcohol syndrome	Lice	Cradle cap
Cystic fibrosis	Lead poisoning	Pinworms	Guillain-Barré syndrome
Down syndrome	Rickets	Scabies	Sudden infant death
Hernias			syndrome (SIDS)
Intussusception			
Neural tube defects			
Patent ductus arteriosus			
SCID (severe combined			
immunodeficiency)			
Spina bifida			

blood transfusion into the circulatory system; or through a break in the skin. In general, bacterial infections are treated with antibiotics, drugs targeted specifically to work against certain types of bacteria.

Viruses are the cause of most common childhood infectious diseases, many of which can be prevented by vaccination (see Vaccination and disease). Like bacteria, viruses enter the body by droplets, ingestion, blood, or breaks in the skin. Some viral diseases can be treated with medicines known as antiviral agents, but viruses are completely unresponsive to antibiotics.

Funguses, plantlike organisms that include mushrooms,

yeasts, and molds, are also a cause of disease in infants. Funguses reproduce by tiny spores that are carried in air or water. If the spores of funguses are inhaled or enter the body through a break in the skin, they can take hold and cause infection. The most common fungal infection in infants is candidiasis, commonly called *thrush*. This infection is treated with antifungal medications that kill the fungus. Fungal infections can become serious and even life-threatening if they are not treated, as they can spread throughout the body.

Congenital and genetic diseases and disorders: Congenital diseases are those that are present from birth but not inherited. These disorders can have environmental, idiopathic (IHD-ee-uh-PAATH-ihk) (unknown), or genetic causes. These conditions include congenital heart defects such as patent ductus arteriosus; spinal cord disease, or spina bifida; and disorders of the digestive system. With increased scientific knowledge and better surgical techniques many congenital diseases and anomalies can be surgically corrected. Infants are remarkably quick to recover after successful surgery. A growing number of surgeries are performed even before birth, while the baby is still inside the mother's uterus. Conditions requiring surgery are diagnosed using ultrasound techniques.

Environmental diseases: Substances in an infant's environment that may be inhaled or ingested may be poisonous or toxic to the infant's body. Lead poisoning, which greatly affects the growing nervous system, can occur when an infant ingests paint chips containing lead.

Parasitic infestations: Although rare parasites can live in or on an infant's body, these are often quickly noticed and removed in the course of the frequent care given to an infant. Danger exists if the parasite is carrying a disease that passes into the infant's bloodstream undetected.

Unknown causes: Among the most frustrating of diseases are *idiopathic diseases,* those with unknown causes. However, an idiopathic disease of today may have its cause and cure discovered tomorrow. Although there are uncertainties about many cases of SIDS (sudden infant death syndrome), it has become clear that many cases have been caused by smothering when an infant lies facedown on a mattress. Putting babies to sleep on their back greatly reduces incidence of the disease.

Wash hands

Get vaccinated

Preventing diseases in infants: Infants are especially susceptible to ingesting disease-causing organisms because they frequently put their hands, toys, and other objects into the mouth. To help prevent infectious disease, bodily cleanliness is key. Special care should be taken to wash frequently the hands of both infants and their caregivers. Using handkerchiefs or tissues when sneezing or coughing, avoiding contact with infected bodily fluids, and properly cleaning or disposing of diapers can also stop the spread of infection. Insects or other potential disease-causing vermin should be prevented from coming in contact with an infant. Foods should be properly cooked and handled to prevent contamination with bacteria or parasitic organisms. In preparing infant formulas, precaution should be taken against using water that could be contaminated with disease-causing organisms or chemical toxins.

All infants need to be vaccinated against childhood diseases (see Vaccination and disease).

Inflammation

SYMPTOM

See also
Abscess
Allergies
Appendicitis
Asthma
Atherosclerosis
Autoimmune diseases
Bowel obstruction
Bronchitis
Burns and scalds
Bursitis
Colitis
Diabetes mellitus, type II ("adult-onset")
Diverticular diseases
Encephalitis
(continued)

Inflammation is a condition of an area of the skin or any other tissue that has become swollen and reddened with excess blood due to infection or injury. It results from the reaction of the body's immune system to damage from an attack on body tissues. Such an attack can include burns, stings, cuts, freezing, sunburn, allergies, and most bacterial or viral infections.

Medical terms for inflammation nearly always end with the suffix *-itis*. For example, appendicitis is inflammation of the appendix, bronchitis is inflammation of the bronchi, and tonsillitis is inflammation of the tonsils.

Cause: Certain white blood cells called *mast cells* flock to body tissues that are being damaged and release *histamines*. Histamines and immune system proteins called *cytokines* (released by cells fighting bacteria) stimulate greater blood flow to the damaged area, bringing redness and fever. They also cause nerve endings to signal pain and capillaries to ooze blood to produce swelling.

Some research suggests that obesity encourages excess inflammation because fat cells release higher levels of cytokines than other cells. This could be a factor connecting obesity to such diseases as diabetes.

Effects: Histamines and cytokines attract white blood cells to the site of damage or infection. Some white blood cells called *phagocytes* help kill invading bacteria. Others release antibodies or chemicals that help rebuild injured tissue. As a result, inflammation often plays a beneficial role in the body's processes for self-healing. The dead white blood cells form pus, which is often associated with inflammation.

Inflammatory processes become harmful when they continue for long periods of time, especially after the initial damage has been corrected. This is the case with rheumatoid arthritis and other autoimmune diseases in which inflammation treats the body's own cells as the enemy. In other cases, such as osteoarthritis, inflammation from prolonged low levels of damage injures tissue. Inflammation has been blamed for nerve damage in multiple sclerosis, for causing plaque and clots in atherosclerosis, and for irritating bronchial passages in asthma.

Treatment: Many nonprescription and prescription drugs relieve inflammation. Among the over-the-counter group are aspirin, ibuprofen, and naproxen (NSAIDs, or nonsteroidal anti-inflammatory drugs) to reduce both inflammation and fever throughout the body; antihistamines for allergies; and ointments and liquids to relieve pain or itching caused by inflammation of the skin.

Abscesses and severe or chronic inflammation should be treated by a doctor. So should rheumatoid arthritis and other autoimmune diseases. Medications for autoimmune diseases may include corticosteriods, prescription NSAIDs, and cox-2 inhibitors such as Celebrex and Vioxx.

Influenza

DISEASE

TYPE: INFECTIOUS (VIRAL)

Popularly known as "the flu," and sometimes called the *grippe*, influenza is a common, highly infectious, usually temporarily debilitating, viral infection of the respiratory tract, primarily the lungs. Other viral diseases called the flu are not, strictly speaking, influenza. Influenza spreads easily from person to person through coughing and sneezing, so it normally appears as an epidemic. Influenza epidemics, for reasons that are unknown, nearly always occur during cold weather.

Cause: There are three main types of influenza virus, categorized as A, B, and C.

- Type C is the mildest. Once an individual has gone through a course of infection and recovery, he or she is likely to have enough antibodies in the blood to resist further type C infections for life.
- Type B is somewhat less stable, meaning it has the potential to change its shape and evade detection by the body's patrolling antibodies; consequently, type B can result in occasional mild reinfection.
- Type A influenza virus is highly unstable; it changes its form, or "drifts," as the phenomenon is termed by epidemiologists (EHP-uh-DEE-mee-OL-uh-jihsts), specialists in epidemic disease. Changes in type A influenza are sufficient to make antibodies developed in response to previous infection irrelevant.

Incidence: Nearly all persons who are vaccinated escape influenza. The CDC estimates that about 10 to 20% of the population who do not get shots develop influenza each winter, but nearly all recover in a week to ten days.

Because it has a long history of developing severe strains in some years, type A is watched closely by national and international surveillance systems, including the U.S. Centers for Disease Control and Prevention (CDC). Each summer, based on the most current data available, an influenza vaccine particular to the anticipated active strain or strains of type A influenza is developed. Persons considered at particular risk—the elderly, those with immune disorders and other serious chronic conditions, and individuals who work in the healthcare field—are urged to get a protective shot. (Persons allergic to eggs, however, should get the advice of their physician first, as the vaccine is grown in an egg-based medium.) Shots are typically administered in early fall to allow six weeks for protection to develop. For people 65 and older vaccination against pneumococcal pneumonia is also highly recommended; it is often available in conjunction with influenza vaccination.

Noticeable symptoms: Influenza is characterized by chills, high fever, scratchy throat, dry cough, headache, muscle

Get vaccinated

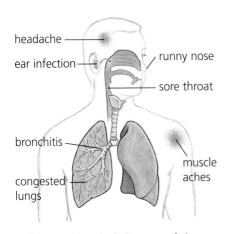

Influenza is a viral disease of the respiratory system, but the fight against the virus produces the symptoms we call "flulike"—headache, fever, fatigue, and muscle pain.

aches, and general fatigue and weakness. Secondary bacterial infections such as bronchitis, pneumonia, and ear infections are sometimes also seen. A seldom seen complication is Guillain-Barré syndrome, a rare form of damage to the nerves that causes muscle weakness in arms and legs. Guillain-Barré is apparently caused by an allergic reaction to the virus. Ironically, it may develop in reaction to an active influenza infection or to the killed influenza virus used to inoculate persons seeking protection from influenza.

The misnamed "stomach flu" (gastroenteritis), which may involve diarrhea and vomiting, is unrelated to influenza.

Diagnosis: Sudden onset of symptoms is a major clue that a disease is influenza. Unless there is reason to suspect some other disease, most physicians will not take blood samples or throat cultures.

Treatment options: Influenza usually is self-limiting and so is treated mainly with bed rest during times of high fever. Antiviral drugs may reduce the symptoms and shorten the length of the illness if given within 48 hours of the onset of symptoms. Antibiotics can be taken to treat secondary bacterial infections if they occur, but they are not effective against the primary viral infection. None of the over-the-counter preparations, such as fever reducers and decongestants, affect the course of the infection, though they may make the sufferer feel more comfortable. It may not be desirable to reduce fever, however, as it is part of the immune process.

History: Influenza tends to produce a strain that is dramatically different from previous ones every 10 to 25 years, resulting in a pandemic, or worldwide epidemic, that is often more severe than ordinary influenza. Pandemics are often given popular nicknames, such as the "Asian flu" or the "Hong Kong flu" (epidemiologists think that most influenza epidemics originate in China). The 1917–1918 "Spanish flu," which also probably originated in Asia, was among the great pandemics of history, killing 20 million people around the globe. About 40% of the American population was affected, and an estimated half million died, many of them young and healthy.

Ingrown toenails

DISEASE

TYPE: INFECTIOUS
(BACTERIAL)

See also
Diabetes mellitus, type I ("juvenile")
**Diabetes mellitus, type II
("adult-onset")**
Foot problems
Leg cramps
Neuropathy

When a toenail curves under and grows into the tender skin of the toe, it can cause a lot of pain. This problem, called ingrown toenail since the nail grows into the toe instead of on top of it, can usually be avoided by good hygiene and well-fitting shoes.

Cause: Ingrown toenails most often occur on big toes. They may result from an injury to the toe. More commonly, they are caused by cutting toenails down the sides in an elongated curve rather than straight across, parallel to the tip of the toe. Another common cause is wearing tight shoes that compress the toes.

Noticeable symptoms: As an ingrown nail cuts into soft tissue around the top of the toe, you are likely to experience pain. An inflammation, with swelling and redness, may develop if the nail is attacked by the immune system.

Treatment options: Soak the foot in warm water to which you have added an antibacterial soap. This will relieve pain and soften the nail and skin. Gently try to pull the skin away from the trapped edge of the nail. If successful, place a thin strip of cotton between the skin and the edge of the nail. This will lift the nail slightly, preventing it from once again growing into the skin. Apply an antiseptic to the infected region daily, and keep the area clean and dry.

If the problem is severe or the area becomes infected, see your doctor. It may be necessary to perform a simple operation, using a local anesthetic, to remove the edge of the nail and some of the nearby skin. To combat infection, antibiotics may be prescribed.

Ingrown toenail is a minor illness in most people, but can be dangerous to persons with diabetes, poor circulation in the legs, or loss of feeling in the legs. Such persons should see a physician if an ingrown toenail develops.

Prevention: Trim your toenails on a regular basis. Cut toenails straight across using toenail clippers. File the corners to eliminate sharp edges. Wear comfortable, nonpointed shoes that provide plenty of room for the toes. Do not wear tight socks or pantyhose, which also can cramp the toes. Protect the toes against injury; for example, it is advisable to wear steel-toed boots if you lift a lot of heavy objects.

Insomnia

SYMPTOM

See also
Bipolar disorder
Clinical depression
Heartburn
Mental illnesses
Narcolepsy
Restless leg syndrome
Sleep apnea

Failure to sleep, or insomnia, occurs when a person spends sufficient time trying to sleep but still does not sleep enough to wake refreshed and able to function. Insomnia strikes older children, adolescents, and adults. Sleep requirements normally decrease with age. Newborn babies sleep 18 hours a day, while teens need only 8 or 9 hours, and the elderly just 5 to 6 hours.

Some people have trouble falling asleep. Others fall asleep easily but wake during the night and have trouble returning to sleep. Some people wake too early in the morning and cannot fall asleep again. At its worst, insomnia combines these problems.

Transient insomnia lasts for several nights or perhaps as long as two to three weeks. *Chronic insomnia* is any insomnia that continues for more than three weeks—perhaps even for years. A change in work shift—from working days to working nights, for example—is often a cause of insomnia. *Jet lag* is another source of sleep loss. In jet lag the internal body rhythms of those who fly long trips from west to east are upset. This upset often produces sleep disturbances.

Related symptoms: People with insomnia often complain of anxiety, depression, and irritability. Other symptoms may include mental confusion (dementia) and problems with concentration and decision making. A person too tired during the day to concentrate may be prone to accidents.

Insomnia may also be associated with other sleep-related disorders such as sleepwalking, sleep terrors, nightmares, and bedwetting.

Associations: Stressful situations, such as losing a loved one, encountering money problems or job loss, traveling, taking an exam, or giving a speech, can all lead to transient insomnia. Common physical causes of transitory sleep loss include heartburn and restless leg syndrome; insomnia in women sometimes appears during pregnancy or menopause.

Chronic insomnia is one of the main symptoms of serious depressive illness, including clinical depression and bipolar disorder. A serious sleep-related disorder that produces insomnia is sleep apnea, the sudden stoppage of breath during sleep. This seldom causes a person to awaken but disrupts normal sleep patterns, producing restless and unfulfilling sleep.

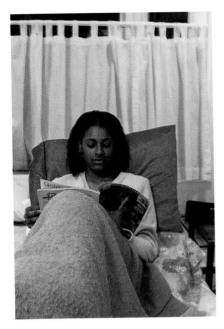

Many people find that if they read a magazine or a book for a few minutes, they relax and then find it easier to fall asleep.

Exercise

Don't smoke

No caffeine

Avoid alcohol

Some other conditions, particularly asthma, ulcers, and the pain of arthritis, migraine, or angina, may cause interrupted sleep.

Prevention and possible actions: If insomnia leaves you feeling sleepy, tired, depressed, or anxious for three or more weeks, see your doctor for diagnosis and treatment.

Sleeping pills may help provide sounder sleep and improve alertness the following day. However, this relief is only temporary, since sleeping pills do not cure insomnia. The sleep that drugs produce is not natural or restful. After taking sleeping pills for a few days, you may feel more tired than ever and think that you need more of the drug. The more you use, the more disturbed your sleep. This creates a vicious cycle called *drug-dependent insomnia.* In one recent study 40% of the people who complained of insomnia were dependent on the drugs they were taking to treat it. To prevent this, physicians seldom prescribe sleeping pills for more than three weeks. For stress-related insomnia, sleeping pills may be prescribed for only a few nights. Physicians do not recommend repeated use of over-the-counter sleeping pills either.

It is not a good idea to become dependent on alcohol to induce sleep. While alcohol relaxes some people enough to sleep, it leads to a shallow sleep with many awakenings. Furthermore, when alcohol is combined with sleeping pills, the result is often fatal, since both alcohol and sleeping pills depress the central nervous system.

Relief of symptoms: Remedies for insomnia include the following suggestions:

- regular exercise during the day, not at bedtime
- no caffeine-containing beverages after noon
- no smoking, since nicotine is a stimulant
- a hot bath or whirlpool before bed
- a glass of warm milk at bedtime
- no daytime naps
- reading a light book (no work-related material)
- a comfortable bed in a room that is neither too hot nor too cold

Some sleep researchers recommend delaying bedtime for an hour or two if you cannot sleep. If you do not fall asleep within 20 minutes after trying this, get up and do some quiet activity,

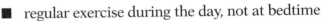

Sleep labs: wired for sleep

Over the past two decades researchers have opened a large number of "sleep laboratories" to study and treat sleep-related disorders. If you go to such a laboratory for a sleep-related problem, dime-sized sensors will be attached to your head and body. The sensors measure and record brain waves, muscle activity, arm and leg movements, and breathing. The physician uses this data about your sleep patterns to diagnose your problem and to prescribe a treatment tailored to your needs.

Treatments include relaxation techniques, yoga, and meditation. Biofeedback techniques are being used successfully in many labs. Bright-light therapy is sometimes employed.

such as reading or working on a hobby. Do not smoke or eat. The next day, whether sleep came easily or not, get up at your regular time, and try to get through the day without falling asleep. Do not let your days and nights get turned around.

Interstitial fibrosis

(IHN-tuhr-STIHSH-uhl fiy-BROH-sihs)

SYMPTOM

See also
Environment and disease
Inflammation
Lungs
Respiratory system
Rheumatoid arthritis
Sarcoidosis
Scleroderma
Silicosis
Tuberculosis

Interstitial fibrosis—also called *pulmonary fibrosis* or *interstitial lung disease*—is a result of certain diseases and environmental exposures.

Parts affected: Fibrous tissue not unlike a scar grows on the walls inside the lungs, which hold the air sacs essential to breathing—*interstitial* means "between the cells" in a medical context. The scarlike tissue, or fibrosis, cuts off more and more of the air sacs. In the most severe cases death results eventually from lack of oxygen or heart failure.

Related symptoms: The person with interstitial fibrosis first begins to notice difficulty breathing after exercise, but as the condition worsens there is continual shortness of breath, a recurrent cough, and a feeling of chest tightness.

Interstitial fibrosis with no known origin is a rare disease, not just a symptom. Not only is there an accumulation of fibrous tissue in the lungs, but also the terminal parts of the fingers, and occasionally the toes, become flattened. Nails curve around these "clubbed" fingers or toes, and the cuticle seems to disappear. This form of interstitial fibrosis often progresses rapidly to respiratory failure and death.

Associations: When some older forms of building insulation or roofing material deteriorate or are disturbed by renovation, tiny airborne fibers of asbestos are released; these can produce interstitial fibrosis. All uses of asbestos in construction have been banned since 1997, and replacing asbestos insulation with less dangerous forms has become mandatory when public buildings are renovated or expanded. Interstitial fibrosis also results from inhalation of other small fibers or particles such as coal dust, silicon compounds, and textile fibers. The general name for lung diseases resulting from inhalation of harmful particles is *pneumoconiosis* (NOO-moh-KOH-nee-OH-sihs) (see Environment and disease). Interstitial fibrosis can also develop from inhalation of irritating or corrosive substances.

Diseases that cause inflammation of the lung, such as sarcoidosis or tuberculosis, can, in the long run, lead to interstitial fibrosis. Scleroderma, an autoimmune disease in which connective tissue turns rigid and hard, can also be a cause when it erupts on the inside wall of the lungs. Another autoimmune disease, rheumatoid arthritis, can have interstitial fibrosis as one symptom.

Treatment: Limiting physical activity can help a person cope with the shortness of breath that is a main effect of interstitial fibrosis. Increasing the amount of oxygen breathed can also compensate for inadequate lung function. Ordinary air is only 20% oxygen, so breathing pure oxygen makes the oxygen five times as available to damaged lungs.

In a hospital, a person may be placed in an *oxygen tent,* an enclosed or partly enclosed region about the head within which the air is enriched with oxygen. If a person is well enough to live at home, he or she may keep a tank of pure oxygen and use it when needed or on a regular schedule. Sometimes a long hose permits continual oxygen enrichment as a person moves about the house.

Prevention: Avoiding exposure to tiny airborne particles and fibers is probably the most important means of preventing this condition. Asbestos removal by trained workers is necessary since ordinary renovation techniques simply spread the fibers. Workers in factories or mines that produce small particles or fibers need to follow work rules and wear masks when appropriate. Smoking tobacco increases the severity of interstitial fibrosis.

Don't smoke

Intussusception

(IHN-tuh-suh-SEHP-shuhn)

DISEASE

TYPE: MECHANICAL

Call ambulance

Intussusception is an alarming condition that develops without warning almost entirely in infants in their first or second year of life. It is a special type of obstruction of the intestine, nearly always of the small intestine. When it occurs, a part of the tubular-shaped intestine telescopes inside a neighboring part, like the finger of a glove that starts turning inside out while a glove is pulled off. *When a child shows signs of having an attack of intussusception, he or she should be taken to a hospital as soon as possible.* When treated, nearly all infants recover completely, but it is otherwise fatal.

Cause: No certain causes have as yet been identified. Some cases seem to develop after recent infections, or at the site of a kind of polyp inside the intestine.

Incidence: Studies indicate the disease is contracted by fewer than 1 in 500 infants. Boys are more susceptible than girls, with the ratio of boys to girls increasing with the children's ages. Although the average age of onset is seven or eight months, intussusception can occur in children as old as six.

Noticeable symptoms: Intussusception typically strikes without warning. In most cases an infant having an attack feels acute abdominal pain that leads to screaming and drawing up of the knees to the chest. The child usually vomits and turns pale as well. Attacks come periodically. Between them the child often calms down and seems to recover. Subsequent and still more severe attacks tend to bring straining to expel fecal matter, which will contain blood and mucus and thus resemble red jelly.

Diagnosis: A physician might first note that the abdomen is swollen and hurts when touched even lightly. The physician also might feel the presence of a firm, rounded mass under the stomach wall on the upper right side.

Conclusive diagnosis is made with a barium enema. In this an enema containing the harmless chemical barium sulfate is given rectally, and an x-ray of the intestinal tract is taken. The x-ray clearly displays the intussusception.

Treatment: In addition to providing a definitive diagnosis a barium enema itself succeeds in clearing up the intussusception of

See also
Bowel obstruction
Digestive system
Diverticular diseases
Gangrene
Small intestine

the intestine in some three out of every four cases that are free of complications. It is thought that the fluid pressure of the enema reverses the telescoped intestinal section causing the blockage.

Instances in which a barium enema fails to correct the condition usually require surgery. In such surgical operations the intestine is manually manipulated to relieve the telescoping. This nearly always clears up the condition completely. Should a part of the intestine become too severely damaged by the condition to heal, the surgeon may remove the damaged section and connect the resulting ends together.

Prompt treatment is important not only to relieve acute pain but to prevent serious complications of later stages. These can include widespread inflammation of the membrane enclosing all abdominal organs, puncture of the intestinal wall, and gangrene.

Irritable bowel syndrome

DISEASE

TYPE: UNKNOWN

See also
Colitis
Crohn's disease
Diarrhea
Digestive system
Diverticular diseases
Gastroenteritis
Large intestine

Another name for intestines is *bowels*. Irritable bowel syndrome, sometimes called IBS, is a disorder of the large intestine that is marked by chronic distress—that is, the illness continues for a long period of time, generally for life. People who have IBS experience intermittent bouts of either constipation or diarrhea, one after the other; the symptoms usually go away between outbreaks. The same person may experience constipation in some episodes and diarrhea at other times. Episodes of lower bowel irritation may also be accompanied by mild pain, slight swelling of the abdomen, and excessive digestive gas.

Irritable bowel syndrome does not lead those who have it to lose weight, develop malnutrition, or become prone to serious maladies of the digestive tract. Only in very rare cases does it seem to become so disabling that it interferes with a person's normal activities.

Other names for IBS have included *spastic bowel, spastic colon, irritable colon syndrome,* and *functional bowel disease.*

Incidence: Some reports indicate that IBS afflicts from 10 to 25% of all persons. More than half of all patients who seek help from gastroenterologists (GAAS-troh-EHN-tuh-ROL-uh-jihsts) (physicians who specialize in the digestive system) come for

IBS. Worldwide, only slightly more women than men develop IBS, but it is much more common in women than men in the United States. Individuals of both sexes typically start to feel its effects in their early adult years rather than as children.

Cause: For people with IBS the colon is more sensitive to stress of all types, including the movement of partially digested food through the system. This reaction tends to intensify contractions, or spasms, of the smooth muscles of the colon that move food wastes through the large intestine. Some of these contractions may produce constipation, pain, and excessive gas. Others may result in attacks of diarrhea. No underlying cause of such abnormal action of the colon muscles has as yet been found.

IBS episodes often follow stressful incidents or emotional upsets. Stress is a common factor in many diseases. Some people react with skin outbreaks, others with stomach upset or heart palpitations, and still others with IBS.

Noticeable symptoms: IBS symptoms may include a puffing out of the abdomen, mucus with one's fecal matter, relief that is brief after passing much gas or having a bowel movement, and even after a bowel movement a feeling of not having emptied the bowel. What tends to distinguish IBS from common digestive upsets is the persistence of symptoms year after year. Symptoms often intensify after eating certain foods, including dairy products, cabbage, beans, and coffee. Some with IBS also have back pain, heartburn, constant fatigue, and faintness.

Diagnosis: Physicians diagnose IBS in part by ruling out diseases that produce symptoms resembling those of IBS, such as colon cancer, diverticulitis, Crohn's disease, or colitis. Tests might include analyses of feces samples, barium-enhanced x-rays of the lower digestive tract, and sigmoidoscopy or colonoscopy (KOH-luh-NOS-kuh-pee), in which an instrument on a long thin tube is inserted through the anus to visually examine the inside walls of the intestine. If sigmoidoscopy reveals an unusually tender colon, it can indicate IBS. In another test a balloon is inflated within the lower colon to detect unusual sensitivity.

Treatment: Increasing the amounts of high-fiber food—whole-grain or oat cereals or breads, vegetables, and fruits—in the diet relieves the effects of IBS in many cases. Foods that are known

High fiber

No stress

to cause symptoms should be avoided. If increased fiber in meals seems to be helping a patient, the doctor may also recommend using a high-fiber diet supplement such as psyllium.

Medicines prescribed may include antispasmodic drugs to help counter irregular contractions of the colon muscles. Laxatives or antidiarrheal drugs may be recommended in periods of special difficulty with constipation or diarrhea.

Reducing stress and anxiety through substance-abuse recovery programs and psychotherapy often relieves IBS. Self-help groups of people with IBS may be formed for group therapy. Individual counseling to reduce feelings of stress may also better the condition. Tranquilizers or antianxiety medications can lessen feelings of anxiety or stress as well.

Use of laxatives, tranquilizers, or other medications should be kept to limited periods of time only. A patient may become overdependent on drugs to regulate bowel movements or stress. Since IBS tends to be a lifelong disease, treatments that can be maintained for a lifetime, such as dietary improvement, are most appropriate.

Ischemia

(ih-SKEE-mee-uh)

SYMPTOM

Ischemia is a condition in which a body tissue or organ fails to receive an adequate supply of blood. Severe ischemia in some parts of the body can require immediate emergency action in order to save a life.

Associations: The experience of having a leg or an arm grow numb after having been held in a cramped position that reduces the blood supply—and having the limb tingle with "pins and needles" as blood circulation returns after the limb had "gone to sleep"—represents a familiar instance of very mild ischemia. Blood supply is nearly always restored to skeletal muscles before any damage is done. When an arm or leg is pinned into one position for a long time artificially, however, damage can occur.

Another mild form of ischemia is familiar to anyone who has had leg cramps after heavy exertion with leg muscles. An insufficient blood supply causes these cramps, which dissipate after a brief rest.

Body tissues die when deprived of blood for more than a few

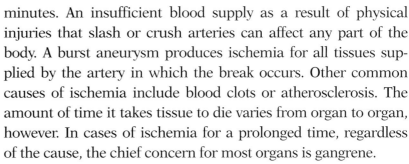

minutes. An insufficient blood supply as a result of physical injuries that slash or crush arteries can affect any part of the body. A burst aneurysm produces ischemia for all tissues supplied by the artery in which the break occurs. Other common causes of ischemia include blood clots or atherosclerosis. The amount of time it takes tissue to die varies from organ to organ, however. In cases of ischemia for a prolonged time, regardless of the cause, the chief concern for most organs is gangrene.

Ischemia in the brain or heart results in serious damage long before gangrene can start. Brain tissue is particularly sensitive to blood supply. The brain or any part of it dies if deprived of blood for only four or five minutes. Heart tissue also dies in a matter of minutes if deprived of blood. Other internal organs can last longer, although destruction of tissue still proceeds in minutes rather than hours. By contrast, the kidneys can go on functioning without adequate blood for an hour or more.

Ischemia of the brain may cause a TIA (transient ischemic attack); the symptoms are headache, dizziness, tingling, numbness, blurred or double vision, or sudden weakness or partial paralysis of one side of the body. Such transient attacks require medical attention because they are often precursors of a more dangerous stroke.

Although the kidneys can last for a time without blood supply, complete ischemia of the kidneys soon leads to renal failure, which is fatal if not treated. Similarly, other organs, such as intestines, quickly develop gangrene with fatal consequences if deprived of blood.

Treatment: In general, restoring blood flow as quickly as possible resolves most ischemia. Surgery is often required. If the cells have died, it may be necessary to remove the affected region. In some cases this may require amputation of a limb.

Sudden slurring of speech or paralysis of parts of the body are common signs of stroke, although other conditions can produce similar symptoms. ***As soon as signs of stroke are noticed, emergency medical help should be summoned.***

Prevention: The major preventive measures for ischemia are those that are usually recommended for healthy living: avoidance of foods high in cholesterol and saturated fats, sufficient regular exercise (especially aerobic), weight reduction if need-

Call ambulance

Exercise

No stress   Eat low-fat foods

ed, and avoidance of risk from accidents. For many a low-dose aspirin daily reduces risk of several forms of ischemia, but such a step should be taken only on a physician's advice, as aspirin can have powerful side effects, including internal bleeding that leads to ischemia. There is increasing evidence that statin drugs, usually used to lower cholesterol, tend to reduce risk of ischemia.

Itching

SYMPTOM

Itching is an annoying symptom of many different conditions. Nevertheless, home remedies or over-the-counter medications are usually effective. In some rare cases itching is a sign of a serious illness. Severe itching is called *pruritis* (proo-RIY-tuhs) in medical terminology.

Parts affected: Itching affects many body parts, although it is always the skin or mucous membrane over those parts that actually itches. Itching is usually divided into two types: with a rash and without a rash (see Rashes).

Related symptoms: Many related symptoms accompany itching. The most common is a rash. Other symptoms include blisters, skin pain, fever, and skin flaking.

Associations: Some common causes of itching are listed below:

- *Allergies,* with or without rashes, are a very common cause of itching. Allergies to food, soaps, cosmetics, and prescription drugs often begin as an itch, then develop into a rash after you scratch them. Prescription drugs may cause an allergic reaction that includes itching.
- *Anal itching,* particularly common in children and older people, has many causes. It usually occurs because fecal material is irritating nerve endings in the anus. Other possible causes include pinworms, hemorrhoids, cracks in the skin surrounding the anus, anal warts, or an allergy to toilet paper. Sometimes anal itching is a sign of a fungal infection, which in turn is an early sign of diabetes mellitus. In rare cases it is a sign of an abscess, polyps, or STD (sexually transmitted disease).

■ *Chronic illnesses* including some forms of cancer and kidney disease can produce itching.

■ *Dandruff* can be accompanied by itching. White flakes falling from the scalp and scalp itching are often signs of *seborrheic dermatitis,* a common yeast infection that inflames the skin of the scalp.

■ *Eye infections* such as pink eye cause the eyes to itch, water, and burn.

■ *Fungal infections* such as athlete's foot cause itching and burning cracks between the toes.

■ *Genital itching,* often called jock itch in males, is most often caused by a fungal infection anywhere on the genitals. Other intense itching can be caused by scabies or by *pubic lice.* In women genital itching, called *pruritis vulvae,* can be the first sign of a yeast infection. In both sexes intense genital itching and pain can be the beginning of *herpes simplex type 2.*

■ *Liver disorders* produce itching combined with jaundice.

■ *Nerve irritation,* known as neuropathy or *neuritis,* often causes pain along with severe itching.

■ *Poison ivy, oak,* and *sumac* are plants to which most people are allergic, so exposure to them causes a severe skin rash that itches intensely.

■ *Ringworm* is a fungal disease that has itching as one symptom, often in the scalp.

■ *Shingles,* also known as *herpes zoster,* is a viral nerve disease produced by the same virus that causes chicken pox. It almost always results in a rash along a long, thin area of the body, following a nerve, and burning or stabbing pain along with itching.

■ *Skin diseases* often have itching as a symptom. These include *eczema, psoriasis,* and *seborrhea.*

■ *Stings and bites,* especially mosquito or gnat bites, are the most common cause of itching, mostly as a result of a mild allergic reaction to the bite.

■ *Sunburn* can cause skin itching, especially when the burned area begins to peel or flake.

■ *Varicose veins* often are accompanied by itching.

■ *Viral diseases* that produce rashes or blisters, such as chicken pox, rubella ("German" measles), or measles (rubeola),

Scratching an itch can damage the skin. Often putting ice on the part that itches will make it feel better safely.

also induce itching, which can be severe in some instances, especially with chicken pox.

Prevention and possible actions: Try to identify which things in the environment cause itching and avoid them whenever possible. For example, many people with sensitive skin can avoid heat and direct sunlight or wear loose cotton clothing if synthetics or wool irritate the skin. Women with sensitive skin should use antiallergenic makeup and jewelry. Check for allergies to cologne, aftershave, or shampoo.

When bathing, use a mild soap or cleansing lotion to prevent skin irritation that causes itching. Pat dry after bathing—do not rub. Use a moisturizer.

Insect bites can be prevented by using a repellent, especially one that contains DEET. It is better to apply repellents to clothing than directly to the skin.

Relief of symptoms: The most important way to get relief from itching is also the most difficult way—do not scratch! Instead, use ice until the itch dies down. Sometimes a cool shower or cold compresses help relieve the itch. Scratching may damage the skin.

There are a number of over-the-counter medications that relieve itching. A well-known one is calamine lotion, which works best for blister itches, such as poison ivy. Oral antihistamines often help relieve allergy symptoms, including itching. Cortisone ointment is often used, but it is important to limit use to a day or two, as cortisone will thin skin and lose effectiveness with prolonged use.

If over-the-counter medications do not work, a physician may prescribe more powerful antihistamines, ointments, or creams. Prescription antihistamines are usually recommended for use in chronic conditions. Pills that relieve itching for 24 hours at a time are now available, as well as more powerful steroid ointments and creams for treatment of psoriasis and other serious skin diseases.

If itching is severe and lasts more than two days, and there is a family history of diabetes or kidney disease, or it is accompanied by the yellowish skin and eyeballs of jaundice, see your doctor.

Jaundice

(JAWN-dihs)

SYMPTOM

See also
Alcoholism
Anemias
Cancers
Cirrhosis of the liver
Congenital digestive system
conditions
Gallstones
Hepatitis A and E
Hepatitis B
Hepatitis C
Liver
Pancreas

Phone doctor

Jaundice is characterized by a yellowing of the skin and whites of the eyes. It is a signal to see a physician. Something has interrupted the normal functioning of the liver, gallbladder, or blood. Babies, especially if premature, often show mild jaundice at birth; this normally clears up in a day or two.

Parts affected: When old red blood cells are broken down, an orange-yellow pigment called *bilirubin* (BIHL-ih-ROO-bihn) is formed. The liver removes bilirubin from the blood and excretes it in bile. Bile is a fluid that is stored in the gallbladder, then discharged through biliary ducts into the small intestine, where it aids in the digestion of fats. If the amount of bilirubin builds up in the blood, the skin and whites of the eyes—which contain numerous small blood vessels—become yellowish.

Related symptoms: Jaundice is often marked by changes in the color of the urine and feces. The urine may darken to brownish green. The feces, which normally eliminate bilirubin from the body, may turn grayish. Itching and abdominal pain may also be present.

Associations: Jaundice may result from any of the forms of hepatitis or from cirrhosis or other liver disorders; in these diseases the liver cells do not transfer bilirubin to bile, thus allowing bilirubin levels in the blood to build up. In obstructive jaundice gallstones or a tumor on the pancreas blocks the bile (biliary) ducts; bile builds up in the liver, and bilirubin is forced back into the blood. Sometimes newborns have jaundice as a result of a congenital obstruction of the bile ducts. Jaundice may also be a symptom in some anemias and cancers.

In *hemolytic* (HEE-muh-LIT-ik) *jaundice* there is an excessive breakdown (hemolysis) of red blood cells; more bilirubin is produced than can be processed by the liver. This process can sometimes come from an immune reaction of a baby to antibodies in its mother's blood, resulting in severe jaundice at birth.

Alcoholism and prolonged alcohol abuse often lead to a breakdown in liver function, resulting in jaundice. Certain drugs may produce jaundice as well.

Diagnosis: A physician will perform various tests to determine the cause of the jaundice. Blood tests and a liver biopsy may be needed if liver problems are suspected. Ultrasound may be used to locate blockages in the bile ducts. Bilirubin levels in the blood will be tested if hemolytic jaundice is suspected.

Jock itch

DISEASE

TYPE: INFECTIOUS (FUNGAL)

See also
Athlete's foot
Fungus diseases
Ringworm
Vaginitis

Jock itch is a minor fungus disease that affects the genital area—its name is short for jockstrap itch.

Jock itch develops most often in warm weather and is contracted mainly by boys and men. Its medical name is *tinea cruris* (TIHN-ee-uh KROOR-ihs) (also known as *tinea inguinalis*— IHNG-gwuh-NAAL-uhs). Its symptoms resemble those of athlete's foot, another disease caused by funguses of the tinea group.

Incidence: Jock itch occurs commonly among males. Some people are naturally more susceptible than others. Girls and women also develop jock itch, but appear to do so rarely.

Cause: Jock itch is not contracted from someone else, as is often the case with a bacterial or viral infection. The fungus causing jock itch is normally present on the skin. When the crotch area becomes warm, moist with sweat, and closed off from outside air for long periods of time, the tinea fungus grows, and attacks on the skin become noticeable. Hence jock itch occurs most often in warmer weather and climates.

Wearing tight underpants or pants or being heavily overweight also increases one's chances of developing jock itch. The fungus thrives in close places where conditions stay moist; this includes any place where two skin surfaces come together. These regions are larger in persons who are overweight.

Jock itch and other fungal skin infections often occur temporarily as a side effect of taking antibiotics. Normally, the balance between harmless skin bacteria and tinea fungus prevents the fungus from multiplying extensively. Antibiotics can greatly reduce the number of bacteria, providing a situation in which the funguses can spread and become more dense. Jock itch caused by this mechanism usually clears up when antibiotic use has ceased, and the skin bacteria return.

Males in whom it develops need not be concerned that it is one of the sexually transmitted diseases. Jock itch develops without any sexual contact whatever.

Noticeable symptoms: The typical symptoms include itching and the emergence of reddish, slightly swollen patches covered with flaky or scaly skin.

Treatment: Most cases of jock itch clear up on their own. Cures can be speeded in mild cases by keeping the crotch area cool, dry, and clean, and by wearing loose clothing so that air can get to the affected area more easily. A traditional treatment is to apply powders that help keep the affected region dry. Over-the-counter antifungal ointments, powders, and liquids are more effective than simple drying powders.

Severe and persistent cases seldom arise. When over-the-counter treatment fails, however, a skin specialist can not only make certain that the itch is caused by tinea but can also prescribe more powerful antifungal drugs if necessary.

Prevention: Jock itch can be discouraged by avoiding the conditions that cause it—such as abnormal heat, sweat, and tight clothing in the groin. It is helpful to attack the problem as soon as it starts, when the fungal involvement is still limited.

Kawasaki disease
(KAH-wuh-SAH-kee)

DISEASE

TYPE: INFECTIOUS (BACTERIAL)

In recent years a number of apparently new diseases have appeared or been identified for the first time. Perhaps the most familiar are AIDS, Lyme disease, Legionnaires' disease, and Ebola.

One of the most mysterious of these apparently new ailments is Kawasaki disease, so named because it was first identified in 1967 by Tokyo pediatrician Tomisaku Kawasaki. It is similar to scarlet fever and probably was often identified as such in the past. Another name for this disease is *mucocuta-*

neous (MYOO-koh-kyoo-TAY-nee-uhs) *lymph node syndrome* (MLNS), which describes its characteristic inflammation of the mucous membranes of the mouth and swollen lymph nodes.

Cause: The disease is caused by exposure to a pair of toxins produced by two different bacteria—one a strain of staphylococcus and the other a variety of streptococcus. The symptoms originate from the immune response to both the bacteria themselves and to the toxins. Scarlet fever, which is a near twin of Kawasaki disease, is similarly caused by immune reactions to a streptococcus bacterium and its toxin, but there is no complication from staphylococcus.

Unlike most infectious diseases, Kawasaki disease does not seem to spread easily from person to person. Therefore scientists suspect that something in the genetic makeup of a victim causes the immune system to react differently to the bacterial invasion. One person may overcome the disease or have mild symptoms, while a small child with a poorly developed immune system and perhaps a tendency toward the disease may become very ill.

Incidence: There are about 5,000 cases annually in the United States. It attacks children younger than six, striking boys more often than girls.

Noticeable symptoms: The illness starts suddenly, with little distress before full onset of symptoms. The patient has a high fever followed by a characteristic rash that may include skin peeling off the arms and legs. The lymph nodes in the neck are generally swollen. Kawasaki disease often produces symptoms common to those of other bacterial infections, including gastroenteritis, pneumonia, and ear infections, depending on which organs are invaded by the bacteria. Joint pain is common.

Diagnosis: The membranes of the mouth are seen to be inflamed when examined under good lighting. The main identifying symptom is a rash on the tongue, known as strawberry tongue.

Treatment options: Once the disease has been identified, it can be eliminated in most cases with a course of antibiotics. Often large doses of aspirin are used to reduce inflammation and help prevent heart complications.

Stages and progress: Like scarlet fever, Kawasaki disease can produce heart disease as a complication, although the form of the heart disease—aneurysms of the coronary arteries—is different from the valve disorders that result from scarlet fever. In 2001 researchers discovered that Kawasaki disease often leaves calcium deposits in the arteries, which increases the risk of aneurysm.

Keratitis

(KEHR-uh-TIY-tihs)

DISEASE

TYPE: MECHANICAL

See also
Bacteria and disease
Cold sore
Common cold
Eyes and vision
Viruses and disease
Vitamin-deficiency diseases

Wash hands

Everyone gets something in an eye at some time or another. Usually, rinsing the eye is enough to fix the problem, but sometimes a foreign body can scratch the cornea, the clear area at the front of the eye, and result in an infection called keratitis.

Cause: In addition to foreign bodies cornea injury can result from wearing contact lenses for too long a period, trauma, or dry eyes. When this happens, bacteria, viruses, or funguses can cause infection at the site of the injury. The most common cause is a virus of the type that causes cold sores or the common cold.

For most people, once a keratitis infection is cured, there is no further occurrence unless the cornea is damaged again. But for some people keratitis can be a chronic, or recurring, condition. In those persons stress, exposure to sunlight, or illness can trigger another infection.

Noticeable symptoms: A person with keratitis may have red, painful, runny eyes that sometimes are sensitive to light. Keratitis can also produce blurred vision.

Diagnosis: A physician will examine the eye for blisters on the eyelid or microscopic ulcers, often after placing a dye on the cornea. When keratitis is suspected, a culture can help identify which kind of infectious agent is responsible.

Treatment: If keratitis is caused by bacteria, antibiotics are appropriate, while different medications fight fungal or viral infections. Eyedrops are usually used to deliver the medicine. In most cases the eye will clear up in a week or two, but if the condition is severe or not treated early, it may take months of treatment. In rare cases scarring and loss of vision can occur.

Prevention: Frequent hand washing, especially when ill, and not rubbing the eyes help prevent eye infections. This is especially important when caring for young children. Properly cleaning contact lenses and not wearing lenses longer than advised are also important preventive steps. A deficiency in vitamin A may promote eye infection, so maintaining a diet rich in orange or yellow vegetables and fruits can be helpful.

Kidney and bladder stones

DISEASE

TYPE: CHEMICAL;
        MECHANICAL

See also
Colic
Excretory system
Gout
Kidneys

Kidney and bladder stones can take years to form and during that time may produce no symptoms. Small kidney stones may even pass harmlessly out of the body by way of the *ureter,* the tube connecting the kidney to the bladder. But a large stone can become stuck in the ureter. Then the patient suffers terrible pain until the stone finally passes, or until a physician breaks up the stone or surgically removes it.

Stones formed in the bladder tend to be larger than kidney stones; they usually are symptoms of such underlying disorders as an enlarged prostate or urinary tract infection.

Cause: Stones begin forming in a kidney when various substances in the urine, such as calcium salts or uric acid, begin crystallizing into small bits of hard material. Over time the crystals grow in size until they become large enough to cause problems. Chronic bladder infections resulting from an enlarged prostate can cause bladder stones to form.

The tendency to form kidney stones runs in families. A tumor on the parathyroid gland also causes stones to form, but this is a fairly rare circumstance.

Incidence: Kidney stones are relatively common and affect anywhere from 240,000 to 720,000 people in the United States each year. About 10% of men and 5% of women will have at least one kidney stone by the time they reach old age. Bladder stones by comparison are not very common, and 95% of the cases occur in men with enlarged prostate glands. Medical experts note that people living in areas of high heat and humidity are more likely to have stones. Calcium stones are by far the most common type, occurring in 75 to 85% of cases.

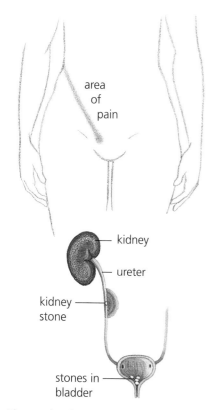

Drink water

The path of pain of a kidney stone follows the ureter as the stone moves or tries to move into the bladder. The side on which the pain develops depends on which kidney is involved.

Noticeable symptoms: Kidney stones sometimes cause no symptoms at all, but when stuck in the ureter, they cause a painful condition called *renal* (REE-nuhl) *colic*. The pain usually begins near the kidney and gradually moves downward toward the groin. The pain comes in waves and can be very intense. Patients with renal colic may also experience a constant need to urinate and notice blood in their urine.

Bladder stones tend to become too large to pass from the bladder with the urine. Patients with these stones experience a frequent urge to urinate, pain on urination, and possibly blood in the urine.

Diagnosis: Because kidney stones may present no symptoms at all, they sometimes are discovered accidentally during routine x-ray examinations. If you have renal colic, your physician will probably order blood and urine tests as well as an ultrasound scan to locate the stones. An *intravenous pyelogram* (PIY-uh-luh-GRAAM), a series of x-rays taken after you have been injected with a substance that highlights the various parts of the kidney, provides another way to locate the stones. The stones themselves do not show up on the x-rays, but the injected substance flowing around the stones reveals where they are.

Treatment options: The first step is to relieve pain with medicine, which may include injection of analgesics.

In recent years a procedure called *lithotripsy* has largely replaced surgery. A machine called a *lithotripter* focuses shock waves on the stones, breaking them up to let them pass out of the body. Ultrasound may be used to shatter stones stuck in the lower part of the ureter. Whether the stones are broken or intact, surgeons often use a small tool called a *cystoscope* (SIHS-tuh-SKOHP), a tube that is inserted through the urethra, to retrieve the stones that do not pass in short order.

Medication can sometimes dissolve bladder stones. Surgeons also may remove small bladder stones with a cystoscope. A procedure called electrohydraulic lithotripsy breaks up larger bladder stones.

Prevention: Drinking six to eight glasses of water a day is a basic measure for preventing recurrence of all types of stones.

Kidney diseases

Infections of the kidney, kidney stones, inherited kidney disorders, and even cancerous tumors interfere with normal operation of the kidneys. Some of these diseases lead to permanent kidney damage and even death.

Among the major kidney diseases are the following:

- *Kidney infection,* also called *acute pyelonephritis* (PIY-uh-loh-nuh-FRIY-tihs), can arise from an untreated urinary tract infection, surgery on the urinary tract, and certain other medical procedures. Infection can lead to more serious kidney problems and be life-threatening to the elderly.

- *Inflammation of the kidney,* called *nephritis* (nuh-FRIY-tihs), *Bright's disease,* or *glomerulonephritis* (GLOM-uh-rool-oh-nuh-FRIY-tihs), usually involves the small ducts in the kidney, the clusters of capillaries in the kidney, or the tissue between them. Acute nephritis sometimes produces few symptoms and usually complete recovery with treatment. In a few cases the disease recurs and becomes chronic nephritis; this can cause progressive decline of renal function—*renal* is the adjective physicians use to mean "of the kidneys."

- *Nephrotic* (nuh-FROT-ihk) *syndrome,* which sometimes attacks young children, is characterized by high levels of protein in the urine and by swelling of the feet, lower legs, abdomen, hands, and face. Severe cases can lead to kidney failure.

- *Inherited kidney disorders* include polycystic (POL-ee-SIHS-tihk) kidney disease and *cystinuria* (SIHS-tih-NYOO-ree-uh). Polycystic kidney disease, which affects about 400,000 adults and ranks among the top five causes of kidney failure, causes clusters of cysts to form on the kidney. With cystinuria tubules in the kidney fail to reabsorb enough of some amino acids (including cystine), allowing the amino acids to be excreted in the urine. This leads to the formation of kidney and bladder stones (see Kidney and bladder stones).

- Inherited abnormalities of a valve in the tube leading from the kidney to the bladder causes *reflux,* the most common urinary tract problem found in children. In this disorder urine flows backward from the bladder up into the kidney. This damages the kidney by creating abnormal pressure and increasing the likelihood of kidney infections.

Cause: Infections and other disorders such as those mentioned above may be brought on by urinary tract infections, allergic reactions to drugs, or even the body's own antibodies that have been produced to fight off an infectious disease such as streptococcal infection, pneumonia, or typhoid fever. A *tumor* may also affect kidney function (see Cancers). Rare inherited kidney disorders also exist.

Serious problems with the kidneys often develop as a complication of diseases elsewhere in the body, such as diabetes mellitus, sickle cell anemia, and multiple myeloma. Kidney function may also be impaired or lost because of physical injury, such as a hard blow to the back.

Kidneys are particularly vulnerable to injury from poisons, as well as toxic chemicals and abuse of some medications, because a large amount of blood constantly flows through them.

Noticeable symptoms: Pain on one side of the body just below the ribs is one of the most common signs of kidney problems. There may also be blood in the urine and high blood pressure (hypertension). Urine may be cola-colored or foamy. Fever, swelling and fluid retention, and weight gain are among other symptoms.

Diagnosis: If a kidney disorder is suspected, analysis of urine will be among the first tests. Urinalysis can help identify whether a bacterial infection, kidney inflammation, or one of the other kidney disorders is causing the symptoms. Other diagnostic tests could include blood tests, a kidney biopsy, an ultrasound or CT scan, or a series of special kidney x-rays called intravenous pyelography (PIY-uh-LAHG-ruh-fee), or IVP.

Treatment options: Whenever a kidney disorder cannot be completely cured, treatment aims at maintaining as much kidney function as possible and alleviating as many of the symptoms as possible. Medication and changes in fluid intake and diet are among the basics for successful treatment.

With more severe disorders the patient's kidneys may fail completely. At one time kidney failure resulted in death, but patients today have two options—regular waste removal through kidney dialysis or a kidney transplant. About 20,000 people in the United States are currently living because of a kidney transplant.

Kidneys

BODY SYSTEM

Shaped like very large lima beans, the two kidneys are an important part of the system for removing metabolic wastes and extra water from the body.

Size and location: Kidneys are about four inches long and two inches wide. Although people normally are born with two kidneys, the body can function with only one. The two are located side by side toward the back of the torso, in the area of the lower back. Each kidney contains over a million tiny filtering systems called *nephrons* (NEHF-ronz). The nephrons are made up of microscopic capillaries that carry blood to be filtered and of equally small ducts to carry off wastes and excess water.

Role: Along with the *bladder* and associated tubes the kidneys are often considered the excretory, or *urinary,* system. Wastes removed by the kidneys are dissolved or suspended in water as *urine. Urine* is stored in the bladder before passing through the *urethra* to leave the body.

Kidneys are also part of the circulatory system in the sense that they remove wastes from blood. They act as endocrine glands by secreting hormones that aid in regulating blood pressure and figure in the body's production of bone and new red blood cells. They also regulate the composition of blood, keeping it from becoming too acid or alkaline, and control the

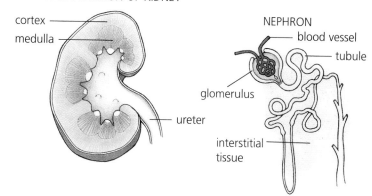

CROSS SECTION OF KIDNEY

cortex
medulla
ureter

NEPHRON
blood vessel
tubule
glomerulus
interstitial tissue

Each kidney contains about 1 million nephrons that do the actual task of filtering waste from blood. The glomeruli are knots of capillaries that bring blood to the nephron.

amounts of certain substances, such as sodium and potassium. The kidneys also produce the active form of vitamin D.

Conditions that affect the kidneys: In addition to various kidney diseases kidney failure, which is the complete loss of kidney function, can be caused by several kinds of acute infection, by reaction to drugs or toxins, or even by antibodies that the immune system has produced to fight off an infectious disease. Other diseases, such as diabetes mellitus, scleroderma, sickle cell anemia, and multiple myeloma, may also affect kidney function.

Labyrinthitis
(LAAB-uh-rihn-THIY-tihs)

DISEASE

TYPE: INFECTIOUS;
      DEVELOPMENTAL

A child who has a severe ear infection begins to experience dizziness and hearing loss. Labyrinthitis is the most likely cause.

Cause: The inner ear, including the organs of balance, is called the labyrinth because of its complex shape. If a person has acute otitis media (a severe ear infection) or any form of meningitis, the infection may enter the inner ear to cause labyrinthitis. A fetus may also suffer labyrinthitis if its mother experiences rubella ("German" measles), especially during the first three months of pregnancy. When caused by exposure to the rubella virus, the condition is known as *viral endolymphatic* (EHN-duh-lihm-FAAT-ihk) *labyrinthitis.*

Get vaccinated

Noticeable symptoms: The symptoms of labyrinthitis are severe vertigo or dizziness. Acute labyrinthitis may be accompanied by nausea and difficulties in maintaining a visual focus.

Diagnosis: A sign of labyrinthitis is jerky eye movement as the head changes position.

Treatment options: Most labyrinthitis is caused by a virus and needs no specific treatment; rest and the immune system resolve the problem in days or weeks at most. Drugs that reduce vertigo are often prescribed to reduce symptoms, however. If a bacterial illness has spread to the labyrinth of the ear, a strong dose of antibiotics is used to effect a cure. Rarely, there is enough damage from infection that surgery is used to drain fluids.

Prevention: To avoid the congenital deafness associated with viral endolymphatic labyrinthitis, women of childbearing age should have immunity to rubella. To prevent the condition in people of any age, all infections of the ear or other parts of the nervous system should be treated promptly to ward off invasion of the inner ear by microorganisms.

Lactose intolerance

(LAAK-tohs)

DISEASE

TYPE: GENETIC

Lactose intolerance is the inability to digest the milk sugar found in ice cream, ordinary milk, and other dairy products. For people with this disorder eating dairy products results in bloating, abdominal cramping, gas, and diarrhea. Similar symptoms occur for some people with other sugars, notably fructose (found in fruits). Rarely, Americans have sucrose intolerance—caused by common table sugar.

Cause: Normally, when people drink or eat anything containing milk, the lining of the small intestine produces an enzyme called *lactase* (LAAK-tays) to break down the milk sugar. With lactose intolerance the small intestine loses the ability to produce enough lactase. Instead, intestinal bacteria wind up fermenting the undigested milk sugar, creating hydrogen gas, acids, and the diarrhea associated with lactose intolerance. Large amounts of sweet fruit, such as grapes, can produce similar symptoms in the fructose intolerant.

While the disorder is most frequently inherited, it can be caused by other intestinal disorders, including Crohn's disease, *tropical sprue,* and *ulcerative colitis.*

Incidence: An estimated 50 million Americans have partial or complete lactose intolerance, including about 95% of Native Americans, 90% of Asian Americans, 70% of African Americans, 60% of Jewish Americans, and 50% of Mexican Americans. About 25% of Americans of European descent other than Jewish Americans are lactose intolerant.

While most babies have high levels of lactase, the ability to produce this enzyme often declines during adolescence and adulthood.

Noticeable symptoms: Abdominal cramps, bloating, flatulence, and diarrhea, the most common symptoms, may appear between one and six hours after eating dairy products and other foods containing lactose. The severity of the symptoms varies widely, however, depending on how much lactase the body is able to produce and how much milk sugar has been eaten.

Diagnosis: Incomplete digestion of lactose leaves various by-products, including hydrogen gas. Hydrogen in the breath can confirm the diagnosis for lactose intolerance. For infants a physician might look for lactic acid in the stool, although it is more common to switch a bottle-fed infant to soy milk to see if symptoms disappear.

Treatment options: Some people restrict or avoid eating milk products altogether. Others use nonprescription lactase replacement caplets, which are taken just before eating milk products.

Large intestine

BODY SYSTEM

Most of the process for obtaining the nutrients from food takes place in long folded tubes called the small and the large intestine, collectively referred to by biologists as the *gut.* Physicians often call the intestines the *bowels.* After most of the nutrients in food have passed from the small intestine into the bloodstream, the remaining material passes into the large intestine. Water is extracted through the walls of the large intestine.

Size and location: The small intestine connects to the large on the lower right side of the body at the bottom of the abdomen. The connection is a few inches away from the end of the large intestine. The dead-end section below the connection is the *cecum* (SEE-cuhm). The *appendix* is attached to the bottom of the cecum.

The main part of the large intestine is the *ascending colon,* which, as the name implies, travels upward from the cecum. When the ascending colon nears the liver, the intestine turns sharply left and becomes horizontal as it crosses the abdominal cavity. This section, the *transverse colon,* passes under the liver, stomach, and pancreas. Reaching the other side of the cavity, the large intestine turns down to form the *descending colon.* The S-shaped *sigmoid colon* centers the far end of the large intestine in the body at the back. A short straight stretch, the *rectum,* leads to the anal opening for waste discharge. Sometimes the rectum is considered a separate organ.

All in all, from cecum to rectum, the typical large intestine is about five feet long.

Role: Virtually the only role of the large intestine itself is to remove water from food residues and transport that water and any minerals dissolved in it into the bloodstream. Various bacteria that inhabit the large intestine further digest food, releasing in the process some of the substances that the body uses. These bacteria also produce gases that form bubbles in the fecal matter; the gases are discharged through the anus.

Conditions that affect the large intestine: While the normal colony of bacteria in the large intestine contributes to good health, certain species or strains of bacteria produce toxins that damage the walls of the intestine. The body reacts to these toxins in several ways. Food wastes may be processed too quickly as part of an effort to rid the body of the irritating bacteria. When this happens, water is not removed because of the short amount of time the wastes spend in the intestine. Feces produced are thin and watery, a condition known as diarrhea. Diarrhea also results if inflammation of the walls of the intestine produces swelling that keeps fluids from passing through. Some viruses can also cause tissues to be inflamed and to swell. Certain parasites, notably amebas, also produce toxins or otherwise halt the operations of the large intestine. A com-

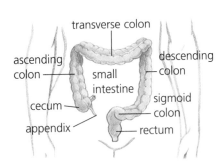

ascending colon — small intestine — transverse colon — descending colon — sigmoid colon — cecum — appendix — rectum

The main role of the large intestine is removal of fluids from food waste. Millions of helpful bacteria usually are present, breaking down and further liquefying the waste matter as it passes through.

mon problem is giardia, in which a parasite attaches itself to the intestinal wall.

Some parasites can live in the large intestine for long periods of time without producing acute symptoms, but they generally debilitate the body by taking energy from it. Among these are tapeworms, pinworms, and whipworms.

The large intestine is also subject to a number of chronic conditions, including colon and rectal cancers. Often such cancers are preceded by small projections of the intestinal lining called polyps. Somewhat similar in nature to polyps but pointed the other way are the pockets known as diverticuli; these are subject to the inflammation called *diverticulitis*. Crohn's disease is thought to be an autoimmune reaction, but the causes of the somewhat similar irritable bowel syndrome and *ulcerative colitis* are both unknown. All three of these diseases produce frequent spells of diarrhea and discomfort; in the case of Crohn's disease the symptoms may be severe enough for sections of the intestine to be removed.

Laryngitis

(LAAR-uhn-JIY-tihs)

DISEASE

TYPE: INFECTIOUS;
      ENVIRONMENTAL

A person with a cold who spends an evening at a game cheering may wake up the next day having "lost his voice." The cause is laryngitis, an inflammation of the voice box, or larynx.

Cause: The most frequent cause of laryngitis is a viral upper respiratory infection such as the common cold. However, laryngitis can result from more serious illnesses, including bronchitis, pneumonia, influenza, pertussis, measles, and diphtheria. Sometimes the condition is brought about through environmental causes, as when the voice is used excessively or when irritating smoke or fumes are inhaled—including tobacco smoke. A sudden temperature change may also lead to laryngitis.

Noticeable symptoms: Laryngitis symptoms include hoarseness or total loss of voice with a tickling, raw feeling in the throat. Usually there is no pain. A mild fever may also ensue.

Diagnosis: On examination the moist mucous membranes of the throat are swollen. Movement of the vocal cords within the larynx may also be somewhat reduced.

Treatment options: The principal treatment is rest, especially of the larynx through not speaking. Whispering to communicate may cause as much damage to the vocal cords as yelling. Home remedies to reduce symptoms include drinking warm liquids, gargling with warm saltwater, using cough syrup, swallowing lozenges, and inhaling steam. Drinking iced beverages and alcohol should be avoided. Care should be taken to eliminate irritants such as cigarette smoke or fumes. If the air in the home is too dry, a humidifier should be used. If a bacterial respiratory infection is the cause, prescription antibiotics will help cure the primary disorder, and hoarseness will soon disappear.

Stages and progress: Hoarseness, usually the only symptom, normally lasts only a short time. However, if laryngitis persists for two weeks, fever is high, or an acute condition exists in children under five, medical care to discover other underlying causes is recommended.

A related, more serious condition is *laryngismus* (LAAR-uhn-JIHZ-muhs), uncontrolled spasms of the voice box usually caused by inflammation. An allergy can cause an even more serious condition called *anaphylaxis* (AAN-uh-fuh-LAAK-sihs); this condition involves, among other symptoms, such swelling of the larynx as to make breathing difficult. ***This allergic reaction to certain foods, medications, or stings requires immediate treatment with the hormone epinephrine.*** A person susceptible to anaphylaxis should always have an emergency supply close at hand and also wear a medic alert bracelet with information about possible allergic reactions.

Emergency Room

Medic alert

Larynx
(LAAR-ingks)

BODY SYSTEM

The larynx, or voice box, contains the two vocal cords we use to produce speech. Muscles and ligaments hold together the nine bits of cartilage that help keep the shape of the larynx. The largest cartilage section, the *thyroid cartilage,* causes the bulge at the front of the neck called the Adam's apple.

Size and location: Just over 1½ inches long, the larynx is part of the upper respiratory system. It lies just below the *epiglottis* (EHP-ih-GLOT-ihs), which is at the bottom of the throat, or *pharynx* (FAAR-ingks), and which closes off the airway when

The complex bits and pieces that make up our vocal apparatus enable human speech. Our nearest relatives, the great apes, lack this complexity and cannot make speech sounds. Damage to the larynx from injury or tumors can make ordinary speech impossible, but modern electronic aids enable persons with damaged vocal cords to produce recognizable speech.

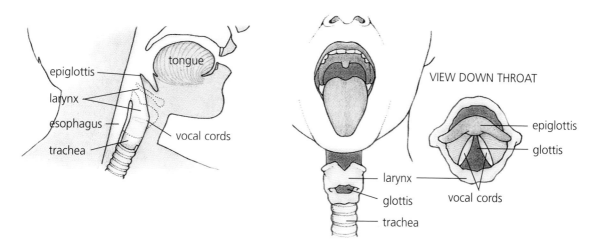

one swallows food or drink. The bottom of the larynx is connected to the trachea, which extends to the lungs.

Role: The larynx produces the sounds we use to speak. Air exhaled from the lungs passes through the *glottis,* the opening in the larynx, and vibrates two elastic vocal cords located on either side of the opening. Muscles and ligaments stretch or relax the vocal cords to produce higher or lower tones. We then shape these raw sounds into speech with our mouths.

Each time we swallow, the larynx moves upward slightly to close the epiglottis, the flap of tissue just above it. This effectively seals off the larynx and the rest of the airway below it. Foods and liquids slide safely past the airway and down the esophagus. Sometimes foods or liquids "go down the wrong pipe" because the larynx and epiglottis have not sealed completely.

Conditions that affect the larynx: Probably the most common condition associated with the larynx is laryngitis, inflammation that causes hoarseness or complete loss of voice for a time. Tumors, both cancerous and noncancerous, can grow in the larynx. Paralysis of one or both vocal cords sometimes results from tumors or other disorders.

Lead poisoning

See also
Colic
Diet and disease
Environment and disease
Poisoning

Acute lead poisoning was first noticed among miners and people who processed lead ores. Today the main concern comes from children's exposure to low levels of lead, which causes a measurable decline in intelligence.

Cause: Metallic lead is not poisonous to touch, but it is dangerous when eaten or breathed. Lead poisoning, however, usually occurs when various lead compounds are eaten or drunk. Lead compounds have many virtues and, despite the danger, are still present or in current use. They can be found in the following:

Old paint: Modern paints are manufactured without lead, but paint containing high levels of lead still coats older buildings inside and out throughout the industrialized world. Such old paint often falls off walls in small pieces. Young children find that paint flakes are somewhat sweet and eat the chips; the result is lead poisoning. Lead compounds from paint also leach into and sweeten soil, encouraging young children to eat contaminated soil.

Dishes: The Romans stored wine in lead jars, and American colonists dined off lead-alloyed pewter plates. Ceramic tableware is considered the largest source of dietary lead today. Some shiny ceramics use lead glazes and decorative paints or dyes based on lead—primarily porcelains or enamels. Less shiny stoneware, unless painted or decorated, has negligible levels of lead. Some glassware, called *crystal,* may contain lead that leaches into drinks.

Plumbing: Studies detect lead leaching from faucets into drinking and cooking water, sometimes reaching levels per pint as high as 25 times the safe maximum daily intake. One estimate is that about 25% of faucets used in the United States leach dangerous levels of lead.

Calcium supplements: Calcium supplements are offered as pills or added to some products, especially drinks likely to be consumed by children. Antacid tablets are also often promoted as calcium supplements. Some sources of calcium are safe chemicals concocted in laboratories, but ground bone and lead-laced calcium-rich earths (dolomite) or minerals (calcium carbonate, also known as limestone) are also used. A study of calcium supplements showed that more than 50 contained lead, 17 of them in amounts higher than the 6 micrograms a day that is

The danger of environmental lead, recognized for centuries, has not disappeared. Old paint containing lead is the most hazardous, mainly to children, but the cumulative effect of lead from plumbing, some ceramics, calcium supplements, or other sources can cause subtle damage to the nervous system.

the maximum allowable limit for children under six years old. Bonemeal-based supplements were the worst offenders.

Occupational sites: Work-related lead poisoning was the first to cause noticeable symptoms. Among the occupations hazardous for lead today are those involved with storage batteries, pottery manufacture, plumbing and heating, machine maintenance and repair, home renovation, and ship or office construction.

Incidence: Fatal lead poisoning is no longer common, but the U.S. Centers for Disease Control and Prevention (CDC) has declared lead poisoning to be the most common preventable childhood disease, with 890,000 children in the United States ages 1–5 having elevated blood levels. However, this is after an 85% reduction over 20 years in the number of children with harmful lead levels.

Noticeable symptoms: Lead poisoning may be *acute* from exposure to a large amount of lead over a short period of time. More often, however, it is *chronic* as a result of many small exposures over a long period of time. Lead is chemically similar to calcium, so the body tends to retain lead with the same mechanisms used to hold on to calcium, allowing small exposures to accumulate over time to toxic levels.

- *Acute lead poisoning:* The mouth and esophagus may react to the passage of a lead compound with a strong burning sensation. There will be stomach pain and intestinal distress, which may take the form of either diarrhea or constipation. As the lead gets into the nervous system, it will produce dementia and eventually paralysis of the arms or legs or both. These will be followed with seizures and complete collapse. Death can easily result.
- *Chronic lead poisoning:* In the beginning there are no symptoms. As lead builds up in the body, it may provoke irritability and loss of appetite. Less obvious changes, such as lowered intelligence in children or hypertension in adults, occur. A higher buildup produces some of the same symptoms as in acute lead poisoning, notably stomach pain and paralysis.

It has long been argued that even low levels of lead in children reduce intelligence. In 1993 a study demonstrated that aggressive treatment of lead poisoning in children results in increased scores on IQ tests at a rate of about one point for each 3 micrograms per deciliter of lead reduction. The most successful treatments reduced lead levels in children with high exposures by 30 micrograms per deciliter.

Moderate lead levels may also damage pregnant or lactating mothers and older adults with osteoporosis. Because lead travels with calcium, 90% of retained lead accumulates in the bones of the body. In pregnancy, lactation, or osteoporosis the harmless calcium is leached from the bones; at the same time, the tagalong and very dangerous lead moves into the blood. From there it can affect various organs, impairing the mind and the operation of the body. Also, the milk of lactating mothers, who are taking calcium from the bones for milk creation, can contain lead in amounts harmful to the nursing baby.

Diagnosis: Blood tests can reveal even small amounts of lead. Since 1991 the CDC has considered levels in blood higher than 10 micrograms per deciliter dangerous. Anemia may be present early on. In adults high blood pressure and damage to the reproductive system are likely at higher levels.

Treatment options: For acute lead poisoning from eating or drinking a lead compound, the stomach is cleaned out by drinking magnesium sulfate or sodium sulfate. For chronic lead poisoning the most important step is to end all exposure immediately. Damage, however, may be irreversible if high levels have already been reached. A treatment called chelation therapy can remove some lead from the body, causing it to pass into urine.

Prevention and risk factors: In most cities lead from faucets and pipes can be minimized by letting water run for a few seconds before using it. However, if lead is leaching from pipes, it may take a minute or two to discharge all the lead-tainted water if the water system has not been used for several hours. When lead pipes are used to connect a house to the mains, as in Chicago, running the water for a short period of time does not help.

If a calcium source is lead free, taking extra calcium along with food lowers rates of lead absorption by the body. Body cells prefer calcium to lead and take up lead only in situations in which calcium is not available or lead is abundant. Good nutrition is important. Lead is more easily absorbed when calcium or iron levels are low or fat content is high.

History: About 400 B.C. Hippocrates of Cos was among the first to document illness caused by lead mining. The modern history of lead poisoning begins in 1723, when drinkers from North Carolina complained that rum from Massachusetts caused them to develop stomach problems and partial paralysis. After Boston physicians attributed the problem to lead parts used in constructing the stills that produced the rum, the Massachusetts legislature outlawed such use of lead.

Around the end of the nineteenth century physicians in Australia discovered that children there were being poisoned by eating paint flakes or powder from painted walls. A few decades later physicians in the United States also learned that children develop lead poisoning by eating paint flakes that have peeled off of interior walls, especially in poorer neighborhoods, where paint is more likely to be allowed to peel. But it was not until 1955 that paints manufactured in the United States began to be limited in lead. The U.S. government finally banned lead in paints in 1978. Old paint was not the only cause for concern, however. Lead solder was used to seal cans of food until 1991. Leaded gasoline, introduced for the first time commercially in 1923, continued in use until 1995.

Effects on world population and health: It is often said that lead poisoning caused the decline and fall of the Roman Empire. One version of this idea is that rich Romans were exposed to lead from plumbing and lead-lined drinking cups, causing the leaders of society to degenerate into madness. Another version has lead used as a sweetener in cheap wine, thereby affecting a broader swath of the Roman population. A more modern twist on this notion is that lower classes in modern industrial societies are less intelligent than upper classes. The reason given is that poor people live in old houses with old paint and in high-traffic neighborhoods with fumes from leaded gasoline.

Such theories are so broad that it is difficult to determine whether they are true. Most experts today think it too simplistic to attribute societal changes to lead alone, although they admit that lead may have been one factor.

Leg cramps

SYMPTOM

See also
Atherosclerosis
Back and spine problems
Cramp
Diabetes mellitus, type II ("adult-onset")
Diet and disease
Hardening of the arteries
Muscles
Parkinson's disease
Skeletal muscles

Nighttime cramps in the leg or foot, called *recumbency cramps,* can wake you from even a deep sleep. These cramps can be painful but usually are harmless, and for most people they do not happen very often. Leg cramps that occur during walking are termed *intermittent claudication* (CLAW-dih-KAY-shuhn). They typically start after walking for a moderate distance at an ordinary pace or after a short distance walking quickly or jogging. Standing still for a few moments causes these cramps to disappear, but the cramps begin again after a similar amount of walking.

Parts affected: Any of the muscles in the thigh, calf, or foot may become cramped during the night. Claudication normally affects the calf muscles only.

Related symptoms: Cramps usually are accompanied by a sharp or aching pain and a slight bulging of the affected muscle. Trying to move the cramped muscle only makes it contract more tightly.

Associations: Leg cramps at night may result from loss of minerals in sweat during earlier strenuous exercise, but often there is no apparent single cause. Some disorders seem to bring on nighttime leg cramps, however, including Parkinson's disease, diabetes mellitus, *spinal cord lesions,* and *hypocalcemia* (HIY-poh-kaal-SEE-mee-uh), a disease associated with calcium deficiency. Patients receiving dialysis for kidney disorders and some types of chemotherapy for cancers also may suffer leg and foot cramping at night.

Intermittent claudication is caused by hardening of the arteries or by atherosclerosis. The arteries in the legs are unable to supply leg muscles with enough oxygen while walking or jogging, especially rapidly. When leg muscles rest for a few moments, the oxygen deficit is made up.

Prevention and possible actions: During hot weather especially, replace electrolytes like sodium and potassium, which are lost when you sweat. Also, try exercising more frequently. Gradually increase your workout instead of trying to do too much at once. This can help resolve intermittent claudication, permitting you to walk farther before developing leg cramps.

If you experience repeated episodes of nighttime cramping,

Exercise

your doctor may suggest quinine sulfate, which is available over the counter. Usually, quinine is taken orally in the evening before going to bed over a period of one or two weeks. Some recent studies have raised concerns about the safety of quinine sulfate, however, so it should be taken only on a physician's advice.

Intermittent claudication is a sign of artery disease and should be reported to a physician. Cholesterol-lowering medications may resolve the problem and may also help prevent heart attack, stroke, or heart failure that could result from arterial disease.

Relief of symptoms: Massaging the affected muscle may relieve the pain and help relax the leg or foot muscle more quickly. Gently stretching the muscle while massaging it also helps. Nighttime cramps usually last only a few minutes and often go away by themselves—standing or walking a few steps often helps.

Phone doctor

Legionnaires' disease

(LEE-juh-NAIRZ)

DISEASE

TYPE: INFECTIOUS
(BACTERIAL)

See also
Bacteria and disease
Lungs
Pneumonia
Respiratory system

A serious illness that leads to pneumonia and other complications, Legionnaires' disease, sometimes called *legionellosis* (LEE-juhn-nehl-LOH-sihs), was discovered after an outbreak of pneumonia at a 1976 American Legion convention in Philadelphia. The Legionnaires' convention gave the disease its name.

Cause: A rod-shaped bacterium called *Legionella pneumophila* causes Legionnaires' disease. The organisms are frequently found in fresh water, but until the 1976 outbreak they had been overlooked by researchers. One reason is that the bacteria live inside other cells, including human cells and tiny single-celled organisms such as amebas and protozoans. As a result, they have been difficult to grow in the laboratory by the usual means—simply growing bacteria on an open food source.

Researchers discovered that the bacteria thrive in the cooling water of large air-conditioning units. The fine spray that air conditioners normally give off during operation carries them into the air. People can then inhale the bacteria. *Legionella* can also contaminate hot-water systems in homes and offices. In addition, dust from construction sites sometimes spreads the bacteria. However, the disease does not seem to spread directly from one person to another.

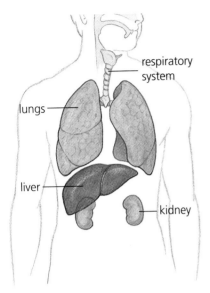

Legionnaires' disease

Legionnaires' disease is a form of pneumonia that may attack parts of the chest cavity other than the lungs. Infection sometimes can spread into the abdominal region. Before the advent of air conditioning and humidifiers Legionnaires' disease was undetected. There may have been occasional instances, but the first known large-scale outbreak occurred in 1976.

Emergency Room

Incidence: Legionnaires' disease can be found in most parts of the world. Many cases have been diagnosed in the United Kingdom and other European countries. The United States has between 25,000 and 50,000 cases a year, about 1% to 2% of all pneumonia cases reported. Though the disease can strike at any time of the year, it is most common from June through October.

Men are two to four times as likely to get the disease as women, and the likelihood of contracting Legionnaires' disease increases with age. Children are rarely afflicted. Middle-aged men who are cigarette smokers and people who have lowered resistance to infection are the most likely to get Legionnaires' disease.

Noticeable symptoms: Early signs include a slight headache, a feeling of malaise, fever, and chills. Other symptoms are a dry cough that steadily gets worse, chest pain, shortness of breath, and muscular pain. Nausea, vomiting, diarrhea, and abdominal pain may also accompany Legionnaires' disease. *The disease is potentially very serious and requires prompt medical attention.*

Diagnosis: Distinguishing Legionnaires' disease from other forms of pneumonia can be difficult. Legionnaires' disease is more suspected when pneumonialike symptoms occur during the summer months. To be certain, a physician will have chest x-rays taken and will send samples of blood and mucus to test for *Legionella pneumophila* bacteria.

Treatment options: Several antibiotics, especially erythromycin or rifampin and erythromycin together, have been found to be effective in fighting the disease.

Stages and progress: Most people recover completely, but a severe bout with Legionnaires' disease can have serious medical complications, including kidney failure and permanent lung and liver damage. For people with lowered immune response or lung function, however, Legionnaires' disease is fatal because of respiratory failure in 15% to 20% of cases.

Prevention: Keeping hot water in institutional plumbing systems at 140°F sharply reduces concentrations of the bacteria. Regular cleaning and use of chemical additives limit or prevent growth of the *Legionella* bacteria in hot tubs, humidifiers, and large air-conditioning systems.

Leprosy

DISEASE

TYPE: INFECTIOUS
(BACTERIAL)

See also
Bacteria and disease
Tuberculosis

Leprosy, also called *Hansen's disease,* is an infectious disease that affects skin, nerves, and mucous membranes. Although its destruction proceeds slowly, it is one of the world's most crippling diseases.

Cause: Leprosy is caused by *Mycobacterium leprae,* a relative of the bacterium that causes tuberculosis. It is probably spread through sneezing and coughing. The leprosy bacilli travel through the air in droplets released when people cough or sneeze. They can survive three weeks or longer outside the human body, in dust or on clothing, for example.

Incidence: Although infectious, Hansen's disease is one of the least contagious of all diseases. Only a small number of people with this disease are actually contagious, and with regular medication they soon become noncontagious. Young men are more likely to develop the disease than women or older persons.

Approximately 95% of all persons have a natural immunity to Hansen's disease. Others, when exposed to the disease, develop a milder form called *paucibacillary* (PAW-sih-BAAS-uh-lehr-ee) (formerly *tuberculoid*) *leprosy.* Paucibacillary leprosy is not contagious, but about 5% of the world population contract the contagious form of the disease, *multibacillary* or *lepromatous* (lehp-ROH-muh-tuhs) *leprosy.* By some estimates as many as one-quarter of untreated patients of the multibacillary variety will become disabled. Hansen's disease has also been one of the world's leading causes of blindness.

The number of infected persons is decreasing rapidly, with the level around the world lowered by over 90% since 1991. By 2001 that meant that fewer than 600,000 persons worldwide were being treated for the disease. However, more than a million are permanently disabled from infection that is now cured. About 6,000 people in the United States have Hansen's disease, and about 100 new cases develop yearly. Most leprosy patients in the United States lead completely normal lives.

Noticeable symptoms: Early signs of Hansen's disease include discolored patches on the skin. Then comes numbness in the discolored patches of skin followed by a gradual but total loss

Phone doctor

of feeling. Sometimes people have attacks of "pins and needles." Some types of the disease produce a rash of bumps on the skin.

Diagnosis: People who experience a loss of sensation in the hands, feet, face, and other skin areas should consult a physician. The doctor will look for enlargement and tenderness of one or more nerves in the affected area. He or she will also do a skin biopsy to check for the presence of the leprosy bacilli.

Treatment options: Several antibiotics are effective against Hansen's disease. A three-drug combination known as MDT is standard treatment. MDT usually makes a patient noncontagious within only a few days, and many are cured in six months to three years.

Surgery, amputation, transplants, or cosmetic surgery may be needed to help patients regain self-esteem. Social rehabilitation is also essential.

The center for research, training, and education on Hansen's disease in the United States is in Baton Rouge, Louisiana. Eleven other regional centers, located mostly in major cities, treat people with Hansen's disease on an outpatient basis and have inpatient facilities in nearby hospitals.

Stages and progress: When leprosy attacks the skin, it destroys nerve endings, sweat glands, hair follicles, and pigment-producing cells. It also attacks peripheral nerves, so the ability to feel light touches and hot or cold goes first. After a time an affected part may lose the ability to feel anything. Injuries, cuts, and burns that patients do not feel become a constant danger. For people with the paucibacillary form of Hansen's disease this is about as far as the disease progresses, and it may even disappear without treatment.

In those with multibacillary leprosy the disease can wreak great devastation.

- *Nose:* If left untreated, bacilli entering the mucous lining of the nose can lead to internal damage, in time causing the nose to collapse.
- *Eyes:* If the facial nerve is affected, one loses the blinking reflex of the eye; this can lead to blindness.
- *Hands:* If the nerve above the elbow is affected, part of the

hand becomes numb, and the small muscles become paralyzed. This may lead to curling or "clawing" of the fingers. Hand surgery and physical therapy can keep fingers flexible.

■ *Legs:* If the nerves of the legs are affected, injury and infection can follow. Over time people with advanced Hansen's disease may need artificial feet or legs, or wheelchairs.

Death from leprosy itself is rare, although the body is weakened and more susceptible to other diseases.

History: Leprosy became epidemic in the Middle Ages in Europe. Yet it was not until 1873 that leprosy could be shown to be infectious rather than hereditary. This happened when Armauer Hansen of Norway discovered the rod-shaped leprosy bacilli, the first bacterium shown to cause a human disease.

People with Hansen's disease have often been treated as social outcasts. In ancient times people recognized that some diseases are contagious. Some contagious diseases with easily seen symptoms came to be called leprosy, although modern writers think that the diseases called leprosy in the past were not the same as the one now known as Hansen's disease. In the ancient Middle East people with disfiguring diseases came to be known as *lepers* and were kept out of ordinary society; they mainly lived as wandering beggars. Scientists who have studied the bones of those people have found that characteristics of Hansen's disease were absent.

Even in modern times people with Hansen's disease have been segregated from the rest of society and made to live in *leper colonies.* Because of the historical confusion between leprosy and other diseases the modern disease is often called by its other name, Hansen's disease.

Attitudes and traditions about leprosy in the ancient world continue to influence the way we think about the disease today. For thousands of years people with Hansen's disease were taken to a priest for exorcism instead of to a doctor for treatment. In the Middle Ages people with leprosy were required to wear clappers or bells or to cry out "unclean" when approaching others. People with Hansen's disease and their uninfected children were banished from their communities and confined in leper colonies. As late as 1913 a U.S. senator who contracted Hansen's disease was forced to resign.

Leukemia

(loo-KEE-mee-uh)

DISEASE

TYPE: CANCER

See also
Blood
Cancers
Environment and disease
Immune system
Lymphocytes
Phagocytes and other leukocytes
Viruses and disease

Leukemia is a general term for various life-threatening cancers that affect bone marrow, the lymphatic system, or other tissues involved in forming white blood cells, also called *leukocytes*. As leukemia develops, it stimulates production of abnormal white blood cells in ever-increasing concentrations. Eventually, the production of abnormal cells interferes with that of other blood components, including red blood cells that carry oxygen throughout the body and platelets that help in blood clotting.

Cause and incidence: Medical researchers do not know precisely what causes leukemia, but contributing factors may include exposure to viruses or to certain hazardous chemicals. Repeated small doses of radiation or a single large dose may also cause leukemia. The leukocytes often display abnormal chromosomes. The disease has been found to occur at a higher rate in some families.

Leukemia accounts for only about 5% of all cancers worldwide, or 10 cases per 100,000 people. Basic types of leukemia include the following:

- *Acute lymphocytic* (lihm-fuh-SIHT-ihk) *leukemia* (ALL) usually affects children and so is sometimes called childhood leukemia. The disease can appear suddenly and cause the body to overproduce immature lymphocytes; these immature white blood cells are called *blasts*. About 85% of all childhood leukemias are ALL, although adults also suffer this disease and in greater overall numbers.

- *Chronic lymphocytic leukemia* (CLL) usually strikes people over 50 years of age. This cancer, which causes overproduction of mature lymphocytes, is the most common type of leukemia overall in Western nations, with an incidence of 30%. CLL is about twice as likely to occur in men as women.

- *Acute nonlymphocytic leukemia*—sometimes ANL, but more often AML for "acute myelogenous (MIY-uh-LOJ-uh-nuhs) leukemia," the most common form of acute nonlymphocytic leukemia—can develop quickly and cause bone marrow to overproduce blasts. AML occurs most frequently in adults.

- *Chronic myelogenous leukemia* (CML) affects the white blood cells called *granulocytes*, causing the bone marrow to overproduce cancerous versions of them. The disease progresses slowly and often strikes people in middle age, accounting for one out of five leukemias in Western countries.

Noticeable symptoms: Acute forms of leukemia often (but not always) manifest symptoms fairly suddenly. Though they may vary according to type, symptoms can include fatigue, headaches, fever, pain in the bones and joints, bruising, abnormal bleeding from the gums or mucous membranes, and swollen lymph nodes.

Chronic leukemias, which progress slowly, may not produce any noticeable symptoms at first. Many times they are discovered by accident through a routine blood test.

Diagnosis: All leukemias eventually result in anemia, fatigue, a tendency to bleed, and an increased susceptibility to infection. CLL can lead to an enlarged spleen or swollen lymph nodes. ALL may cause swelling of the lymph nodes, spleen, or liver. Serious and rapidly developing anemia characterizes AML.

Blood tests and biopsy of the bone marrow—examination of sample bone marrow under a microscope—are the surest ways to diagnose leukemia and to determine its type.

Treatment options: Chemotherapy, often in combination with radiation and bone marrow transplants, has been used with varying degrees of success in treating leukemias. Bone marrow transplants provide a source of noncancerous cells that produce normal leukocytes. Because high doses of chemotherapy may kill bone-marrow cells, a combination of aggressive chemotherapy followed by a bone-marrow transplant is often the key to successful treatment.

Other forms of treatment are being researched, including use of vitamin A, treatment with alpha interferon, and transplant of umbilical cord blood collected during normal births. Cord blood contains stem cells that are progenitors of all blood cells.

Stages and progress: Whether the leukemia progresses slowly or quickly, it is fatal without successful medical treatment. Treatment, however, often arrests or eliminates the disease, and today the five-year survival rate for leukemia patients is 42%, three times what it was in the 1960s.

Lice

DISEASE

TYPE: PARASITIC

See also
Parasites and disease
Typhus

Lice, commonly called cooties or crabs, are so small that it is hard to see them without a magnifying glass. They can live on any part of the body that has hair, where they cement clusters of eggs to the hair shafts.

Cause: Three species of tiny insects called lice affect humans. *Pediculosis capitis* (puh-DIHK-yuh-LOH-sihs KAAP-uh-tihs), or head lice, infest the scalp. *Pediculosis corporis* (KAWR-puhr-ihs), body lice, inhabit clothing and bedding. *Pediculosis pubis* (PYOO-bihs), pubic lice, are found in the pubic hair around the genitals.

Lice are often called crabs because they look like tiny crabs. They are a bit more than one-sixteenth inch long, the size of a sesame seed. Their tiny, white, elongated eggs are called nits; the eggs hatch into larvas. All three generations—nits, larvas, and adults—can be found on the body at the same time.

Lice feed on human blood and move from place to place by crawling. They attach to the skin of the human host and bite to suck out the blood.

Incidence: Outbreaks of head lice occur frequently among young children in day-care centers, elementary schools, and day camps. Body lice often are associated with lack of cleanliness; they tend to be found in clothing that is not cleaned regularly. Pubic lice are usually passed from one person to another during intimate sexual contact.

Noticeable symptoms: Intense itching at the area of infestation is usually the first sign that a person has lice. The person may also notice the lice themselves or clusters of nits attached to body hairs. A handheld magnifying glass makes them easier to see.

Diagnosis: A physician may diagnose lice infestation by observing lice or nits or by observing puncture marks where the lice have fed.

Treatment options: Body and pubic lice infestations are usually treated with medicated lotions. Some lotions can be purchased over the counter, but others require a prescription. Lotion is applied liberally to cover the affected area and left on overnight. It is then washed off and clean clothing is put on. Medicated shampoos are used to eliminate head lice; a special comb, called a nit comb, can help remove the eggs. To be sure that all stages of the louse life cycle are destroyed, the treatment is repeated after seven to ten days.

Lice and their eggs sometimes get into the eyebrows and eyelashes. Petroleum jelly rather than medicated lotion is used to destroy lice in these sensitive areas.

All clothing, towels, and bedding that the infested person had contact with should be washed in hot water and dried in a dryer; clothes that must be dry-cleaned should be placed in a bag labeled "lice infested" before taking them to the cleaners. All individuals in a household should be treated at the same time to prevent any further spread.

Antibiotics may be prescribed if scratching the infestations has caused an infection.

Stages and progress: It can take two to three weeks after lice inhabit the body before intense itching begins. This is the length of time it takes the eggs to hatch and grow into adults. Although body lice can carry typhus, a serious disease, the most common complication of untreated lice infestation is secondary infection caused by scratching too hard.

Prevention: Head lice in children are very common. It is important to look for lice and nits whenever a child scratches his or her head a lot. If lice are found, notify the public health department or school so that an outbreak can be prevented.

Body lice can be prevented by good housekeeping practices and regular bathing. Thorough, frequent cleaning of clothing and linens reduces the likelihood of body lice infestations. Sharing only clean clothing can reduce the possibility of lice finding new hosts.

Pubic lice are more of an embarrassment than a health hazard. Prompt treatment of all sex partners will prevent the spread to others.

Ligaments

BODY SYSTEM

Bones usually attach to each other with somewhat flexible tissues called ligaments, which are similar to narrow sheets of tough plastic.

A few bones, such as those in the skull, form rigid attach-

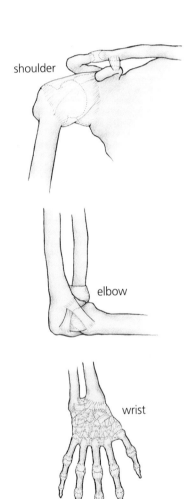

shoulder

elbow

wrist

Covering joints

The ribbons of ligament overlap at a joint, protecting it as well as holding the bones together.

ments instead of being held together by ligaments. Every place that two bones connect with each other, whether by fusing together or by flexible ligaments, is a *joint*.

Size and location: Ligaments are found at all joints where two bones can move. Sometimes movement is relatively free, as in the shoulder, and sometimes quite restricted, as in rib joints. Usually, several ligaments overlap at each joint, surrounding the joint on all sides.

Ligaments are made chiefly of *collagen*. Most are white and do not stretch easily. The only ligaments that are truly elastic are yellow ones found in the neck, yellow because they are made from the protein elastin as well as collagen. Elastin enables yellow ligaments to stretch.

Role: Ligaments hold the skeleton together and also provide the outer surfaces of some joints. Inside the covering ligaments a smooth membrane and lubricating liquid allow movable joints freedom of movement. In some cases the ligaments have a role beyond connection or coverage. For example, ligaments shape the arch of the foot. The ligaments of the arch are the shock absorbers of the body, acting like automobile shock absorbers in reducing jolts and jars of locomotion. Ligaments also help shape the breasts and support some internal organs, such as the liver, uterus, and bladder.

Conditions that affect the ligaments: The main problem that affects ligaments is overextension as a result of moving a joint in the wrong direction or moving it farther than the nonelastic ligament allows. Damage to ligaments that occurs from this cause is called a *sprain*. A minor *strain* may involve stretched ligaments, but when the ligaments tear, healing time increases. Tennis elbow often consists of a minor sprain along with inflammation of the tendon where it is attached to a ligament.

For reasons that are poorly understood, collagen is sometimes attacked by the immune system. In one of the most common collagen diseases, lupus (systemic lupus erythematosus), the immune system often attacks the collagen in ligaments, producing arthritis that is similar to rheumatoid arthritis. In rheumatoid arthritis, however, the attack is on the membrane between joints rather than on the ligaments.

Listeriosis

(lih-STEHR-ee-OH-sihs)

DISEASE

TYPE: BACTERIAL

See also
Bacteria and disease
Blood poisoning
Endocarditis
Food poisoning
Gastroenteritis
Meningitis
Pneumonia

Phone doctor

Every day thousands of people choose to lunch on a turkey sandwich because is it lower in fat than many other lunch choices and therefore better for their health. But in the spring of 2000, 29 people in 10 states came down with a food-borne illness called listeriosis from eating turkey-based lunchmeat from a source infected with *Listeria*.

Cause: Listeriosis is caused by the bacterium *Listeria monocytogenes,* found naturally in soil and water. Farm animals can become infected while feeding outdoors; they remain healthy, but their meat or milk or both can contain *Listeria*.

People get listeriosis by eating food contaminated with *Listeria*. The usual sources are unpasteurized milk or products made with unpasteurized milk, soft cheeses, raw seafood, and processed foods such as lunchmeat or hot dogs made and packaged in contaminated facilities.

Incidence: Each year in the United States there are about 2,500 cases of listeriosis. Of these, about 500 are fatal. People with healthy immune systems can be infected with *Listeria* without becoming seriously ill, but pregnant women, newborns, people with diabetes or kidney disease, the elderly, and those with damaged immune systems may experience serious illness. Listeriosis can also damage or kill a fetus when a pregnant woman becomes infected.

Noticeable symptoms: Fever, muscle aches, and sometimes diarrhea or nausea (gastroenteritis) are the most common early symptoms of listeriosis. If the infection leads to meningitis, headache, stiff neck, loss of balance, and convulsions may occur.

Diagnosis: When reported symptoms suggest listeriosis, a blood test or spinal fluid test is used to confirm the diagnosis.

Treatment: Antibiotics are used to treat listeriosis, but the disease progresses rapidly and is fatal in about 20% of diagnosed cases. The most serious problems are bacterial meningitis, blood poisoning (sepsis), pneumonia, and endocarditis.

Prevention: People in any of the risk categories for listeriosis—such as pregnant women—should reduce the chance of infection by avoiding any foods likely to contain *Listeria*. It is also important to pay attention to announcements of food recalls and to quickly report any symptoms to a physician.

Liver

BODY SYSTEM

See also
Abscess
Alcoholism
Cancers
Cirrhosis of the liver
Drug abuse
Environment and disease
Gallstones
Hepatitis A and E
Hepatitis B
Hepatitis C
Jaundice
Malaria
Parasites and disease
Poisoning
Wilson's disease

The liver is the main chemical factory of the body and, after the skin, the largest organ in the body.

Size and location: The liver is a large dark red mass that can be separated into four distinct chunks, called *lobes*. Each lobe is about the same in most ways although somewhat different in size. Beyond the lobes and some fatty tissue that separates them, most of the liver appears to be an undivided mass. It weighs some three to four pounds, considerably more than the heart, stomach, or lungs, the other large organs of the abdominal cavity. In a living person the liver actually weighs more than that because it is filled with blood—at any one time from 25 to 30% of all the blood in the body is in the liver.

The liver is located near the top of the abdomen below the diaphragm. It is normally high enough to be surrounded by the lower ribs. Below the liver the stomach and intestines fill most of the remainder of the lower abdomen.

Role: If, for some reason, a person loses liver function completely, death follows within a day. Thus the liver is a *vital organ* like the heart or lungs—necessary for life. Unlike the heart or lungs, however, each of which performs essentially a single task, the liver is engaged in a wide variety of functions. As part of the digestive system, the liver acts as a ducted or exocrine gland that produces *bile*, a substance that helps reduce the acidity of the nutrient mixture and also helps break down fats with a detergent action. The liver is also part of the circulatory system, since it cleans poisons out of the blood and regulates blood's composition in various other ways. The liver also scavenges unwanted chemicals from the blood, takes them apart, and reassembles the parts into needed chemicals or into wastes.

Among the important chemicals produced by the liver are *cholesterol*, which, despite its unsavory reputation, is necessary for life as it is the chief component of all cell membranes; *glycogen*, the starchlike substance used to store sugary glucose for use when needed; *urea,* the form in which wastes from nitrogen compounds, such as proteins and DNA, are prepared to leave the body; vitamin A; and blood proteins that are used in clotting.

Conditions that affect the liver: The liver is subject to infection by bacteria and some parasites, but the most common liver infections are from several different viruses; the diseases caused by viral liver infections are all called hepatitis, as are other conditions, including chemical poisoning, that produce liver inflammation. Parasites include worms called *flukes* and protists called *amebas.* Liver parasites tend to be problems of underdeveloped regions.

The liver is subject to abscesses. Chronic inflammation of the liver leads to a condition called cirrhosis, in which liver cells are displaced by fat and scar tissue.

Almost any disease that seriously affects liver function can be recognized by jaundice, a yellowish cast to skin and eyes that is produced when the liver cannot process used red blood cells.

Although stones do not form in the liver itself, they often form from cholesterol in the gallbladder. If the stones plug the passage of bile from the liver through the gallbladder to the stomach, the liver is affected by its own bile backing up into the cells.

Chemicals of one kind or another may prove to be more powerful than the liver's ability to convert them to harmless substances. In that case the chemicals may damage the liver. Harmful chemicals range from hydrocarbon vapors to ethyl alcohol, the active ingredient in beer, wine, and liquor. Most people do not drink enough alcohol at one time to cause acute alcohol poisoning, but many drink enough for long periods of

The liver in antiquity

Writers from ancient Greece and Rome recognized three principal organs, the heart, the brain, and the liver—and often the liver seemed to be the most important. Their medicine was based on four fluids called *humors:* blood, phlegm, yellow bile (choler), and black bile—two out of the four apparently productions of the liver. Whichever humor dominated determined whether a person was sanguine (with blood dominating), phlegmatic, choleric, or bilious. Although the concept survived well into the sixteenth century, it was based on many errors. Most striking is that there is only one color of bile. Fresh bile may be somewhat more yellowish than older, blacker bile, but it is all just liver bile.

time to produce cirrhosis of the liver. Nearly half of all instances of liver cirrhosis stem from alcohol abuse.

Cancers rarely begin in the liver in the West, but liver cancer spread from elsewhere in the body is a common form of cancer that is nearly always fatal. In Asia and Africa diseases or environmental conditions make cancers originating in the liver more common.

Among the astonishing feats of the liver is its power to regrow from small pieces of itself. While some organisms can regenerate a lost tail or even, in the case of starfish, a whole body from a part, the liver is the only internal organ in humans that can accomplish this feat. Even with the power of regeneration the liver is often defeated by its many enemies. As a result, death from liver diseases is currently eleventh in frequency among fatalities in the United States.

Lockjaw	*See* **Tetanus**
Lower back pain	*See* **Back and spine problems**

Lung cancer

DISEASE

TYPE: CANCER

Lung cancer is the leading cause of cancer deaths in the United States. Yet the majority of these deaths could be prevented if people avoided the use of tobacco products.

There are several varieties of lung cancer. For treatment purposes these are usually classified in two groups: small cell lung cancer and non-small cell lung cancer.

Cause: Cigarette smoking is the major cause of lung cancer, estimated to be responsible for 87% of all lung cancer deaths. Tobacco smoke contains thousands of chemicals, many of which are known carcinogens. The average smoker is thus subjected to a constant barrage of hazardous agents. Other contributors to lung cancer include exposure to environmental ("second-hand") tobacco smoke, air pollution, airborne asbestos, radiation, and radon (a radioactive gas that can enter homes through foundation cracks and drinking water).

Incidence: About 170,000 new cases of lung cancer are diagnosed in the United States each year, accounting for 13% of new cancer cases. The disease has a high death rate, with about 157,000 deaths annually in the United States. Lung cancer is also the leading cause of cancer death in most other countries.

Lung cancer is rare before age 40 and most common after age 60. Incidence rates are higher among men than women. This reflects the fact that cigarette smoking has long been more prevalent among men than women.

Noticeable symptoms: The earliest and most common symptom of lung cancer is a chronic cough. Other symptoms may include wheezy breathing, shortness of breath, coughing up of blood, and chest or shoulder pain. Recurring bronchitis or pneumonia also may indicate the presence of lung cancer. If the cancer has spread to other parts of the body, such as the liver or bones, pain may occur in these sites, and the patient may experience noticeable weight loss.

Diagnosis: A chest x-ray will be taken to look for shadows that indicate the likely presence of cancer. To confirm a diagnosis, additional tests will be conducted, including analysis of cells in the patient's sputum (mucous secretions from the lungs) and perhaps visual inspection and a biopsy of the lining of the bronchi by inserting an instrument called a bronchoscope into the lungs.

It also is important to determine the type of lung cancer. Small cell lung cancer spreads rapidly and often is widespread by the time it is diagnosed. Non-small cell lung cancer is less likely to have spread at the time of diagnosis.

Stages and progress: There are few pain nerves in the lungs, so cancers often grow for many years before discovery—five to ten years on average. Following diagnosis, the patient is assigned a "stage." This enables a physician to choose the most effective treatment. Staging describes the size of the tumor and whether it has *metastasized* (muh-TAAST-uh-SIYZD), or spread to bones and distant parts of the body. The larger the tumor and the farther it has spread, the more difficult it is to treat. If the cancer is localized in the lung, the five-year survival rate is 49%. But few lung cancers are discovered that early. The overall five-year survival rate for lung cancer is only 14%.

Treatment options: If lung cancer is diagnosed while it is still localized in one lung, a surgeon may remove all or part of the lung. For advanced cases, including cancers that have spread, radiation, chemotherapy, or some combination of the two generally is used to try to shrink the tumors.

Prevention and risk factors: Avoiding the use of tobacco greatly reduces the risk of lung cancer. The risk of dying from lung cancer is more than 20 times higher among male smokers and 12 times higher among female smokers than among people who have never smoked. People who quit smoking, particularly if they do so before age 50, decrease their risk of lung cancer and other diseases; the earlier they quit, the greater the benefits. Avoiding exposure to other risk factors, including environmental tobacco smoke, also significantly protects against lung cancer.

Lungs

BODY SYSTEM

Lungs are two elastic sacs that form the most important organ of the respiratory system. When you inhale, the muscles of your diaphragm contract, causing both lungs to expand and take in fresh air; when you exhale, they relax, allowing the lungs to contract and force used air and carbon dioxide out. Each day you inhale and exhale the equivalent of about 5,000 gallons of air.

Size and location: Located on either side of the heart, each lung is enclosed in an airtight sac called the *pleural membrane*. Air enters a lung through a *bronchus* (BRONG-kuhs; plural *bronchi*—BRONG-kiy). The bronchus divides into smaller *bronchial tubes*, which continue to divide until they become very fine tubes called *bronchioles*. Each bronchiole ends in a cluster of tiny round bodies called an *air sac*. As small as air sacs are, each of the round bodies contains even smaller cavities called *alveoli*. Adults have as many as 300 million alveoli in their lungs. The two lungs together weigh about 1.3 pounds.

Role: Lungs perform the crucial jobs of transferring oxygen from the air to the bloodstream and of filtering carbon dioxide, a waste product from metabolism, out of the blood. It is in the thin-walled alveoli that the exchange of oxygen to and carbon dioxide from the blood actually takes place. Although each alveolus is tiny, the total surface area the alveoli present is about 40 times the surface area of the skin, enabling blood vessels surrounding

Heart and lungs

Although we think of both lungs as being essentially the same, the right lung is substantially larger than the left. This allows a space for the heart. For some illnesses the cure is a transplant of the heart and lungs together as a unit.

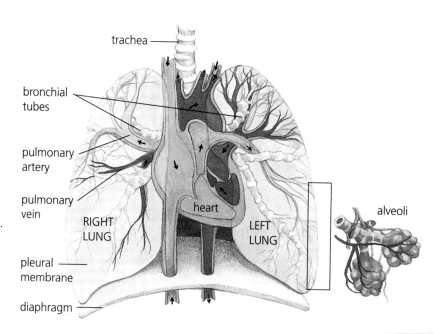

trachea

bronchial tubes

pulmonary artery

pulmonary vein

RIGHT LUNG

heart

LEFT LUNG

alveoli

pleural membrane

diaphragm

each of these sacs to absorb the oxygen. Carbon dioxide passes from the blood vessels into the alveoli so that it can be exhaled. Lungs also filter and remove foreign matter from the air.

Conditions that affect the lungs: Because the lungs are so important, disorders that affect them can be very serious. Bacteria and viruses cause infectious diseases of the lungs, including acute bronchitis, pleurisy, and tuberculosis. Funguses also invade the lungs with serious consequences. A lung abscess, a pus-filled area in the lung, may be a complication of one of these diseases.

Whenever lungs fill with fluid instead of gases, a condition called *pulmonary edema,* breathing is impaired and may halt altogether. Various forms of pneumonia occur when the alveoli become inflamed and fill with pus and other liquids. Hantavirus is another cause of fluid-filled lungs; it is produced when the virus causes plasma to pass through cell walls. Heart disease can also fill lungs with fluid.

Cystic fibrosis is an inherited disease that affects the lungs. Asthma may be caused by allergic reactions, and breathing air filled with certain types of particles over a long period may lead to diseases such as *asbestosis* (AAS-behs-TOH-sihs) and silicosis. Cigarette smoking is the primary cause of lung cancer; it also contributes to COPD (chronic obstructive pulmonary disease) and emphysema.

A stab wound that punctures a lung can cause the lung to collapse, called *pneumothorax* (NOO-moh-THAWR-aaks). The lung will not expand and contract normally until the puncture has been sealed.

"Lupus" (systemic lupus erythematosus)

(LOO-puhs EHR-uh-THEE-muh-TOH-suhs)

DISEASE

TYPE: AUTOIMMUNE

The butterfly rash is the origin of the name of the disease lupus, since it resembles markings on the face of a wolf (*lupus* in Latin).

Systemic lupus erythematosus—usually just called lupus or *SLE*—is one of the autoimmune diseases.

Cause: The body's immune system generates antibodies not only to invading microorganisms but also to some of the body's own cells, as if they, too, were foreign invaders to be hunted down and destroyed. Often such an autoimmune reaction begins with a viral disease. Lupus tends to be concentrated in certain families and ethnic groups, a sign of genetic influence.

Incidence: The general incidence of lupus is about 7 in every 100,000, but it is higher in certain ethnic groups. About 90% of those who have lupus are women, and the disease usually makes its first appearance in early adulthood.

Noticeable symptoms: Symptoms of lupus are likely to occur in periodic episodes called flares, and they vary widely from person to person. The most characteristic symptom is the reddish, butterfly-shaped rash on the nose and cheeks. Other common symptoms are fatigue, arthritis, and fever.

Diagnosis: Lupus is difficult to distinguish from other diseases, partly because its symptoms are so varied and partly because tests for characteristic antibodies in the blood are sometimes inconclusive. Diagnosis must often be based on a combination of observed signs and symptoms, evidence of physical damage in organs such as the heart or kidneys, and the results of blood tests.

Stages and progress: Lupus may affect several different organs or body systems, producing widely varying symptoms. Unless organs such as the kidneys are seriously damaged, lupus is seldom life-threatening. Otherwise, the effects are as variable as the symptoms. Some of those affected may find flareups to be no more than a periodic nuisance, while others may be seriously incapacitated during episodes or even most of the time.

- *Skin:* Reddish rashes may appear on various parts of the body, but most often on the face. The butterfly-shaped rash on the cheeks and across the nose is frequently triggered by exposure to sunlight, to which the skin is unusually sensitive. Hair loss is fairly common on the head or the body or both.

- *Joints and muscles:* Painful inflammation of one or more joints is especially common and may cause the disease to be mistaken for rheumatoid arthritis.

- *Mouth:* Painfully inflamed sores, or ulcers, may appear on the mucous membranes lining the mouth or throat.

- *Blood:* Several types of blood cells may be reduced in number, causing anemia from fewer red blood cells. Reduced white cells make the body more vulnerable to infection. Insufficient platelets prevent the blood from clotting properly and can lead to dangerous bleeding. In addition, blood vessels may be blocked by inflammation and damaged cells.

- *Heart:* The membrane surrounding the heart, the pericardium, may become inflamed, a condition called pericarditis. Irregular heartbeats, or arrhythmias, are common, and the risk of coronary heart disease is higher than usual.

- *Chest:* The membrane lining the chest cavity may be inflamed, a condition called pleurisy. Chest pain and breathing difficulties may also be caused by muscle damage.

- *Brain:* During flares affected individuals may suffer from headaches, seizures, or personality changes.

- *Kidneys:* The narrow passageways within the kidneys may become clogged and inflamed by complexes of antibodies and the cell components they are attacking. The effects may eventually become severe enough to cause kidney failure.

- *Reproductive system:* Women with lupus run a higher than normal risk of miscarriage and premature birth, and their babies may be abnormally small or have a treatable heart defect called *congenital heart block.*

Treatment options: During flares various agents are used to fight the inflammation that underlies many of the symptoms. Corticosteroids may be effective but they can have undesirable or even dangerous side effects, such as increased risk of infection. At present most doctors make only limited use of them and often prescribe antibiotics along with them to head off infection. Milder nonsteroidal anti-inflammatory drugs (NSAIDs) such as aspirin and ibuprofen are often used instead. Some physicians are trying cox-2 inhibitors (Celebrex and Vioxx are best known), which have fewer side effects than NSAIDs. For unknown reasons drugs originally used to fight malaria also tend to prevent lupus flares.

Very serious attacks, especially those involving the kidneys, may be halted with drugs that suppress the immune system. These, too, raise the risk of infection and may have to be accompanied by antibiotics.

Lyme disease

DISEASE

TYPE: TICK-BORNE
(BACTERIAL)

See also
Animal diseases and humans
Bacteria and disease
Bell's palsy
Rashes

People who go into the woods or who work or play near bushes can get Lyme disease. With care this serious disease can be prevented.

Cause: Lyme disease is caused by a bacterium that is transmitted by bites from a tick, usually a type called a blacklegged tick (also known as a deer tick). Deer and white-footed mice are the principal sources of the bacterium and are also prey to the ticks. Only about 1 tick bite in 20 leads to the disease in humans. The disease is not transmitted in any other way and cannot be caught from another person. Despite this, Lyme disease is a major problem in many parts of the United States.

Incidence: By 2000 the number of reported Lyme disease cases had reached over 17,000 in the United States and was still climbing at a rate of 8% a year. Authorities believe that reported cases are the tip of the iceberg, with as many as 9 cases undiagnosed for every one reported.

Lyme disease is concentrated in suburban regions in the U.S. Northeast, especially Connecticut, Rhode Island, New Jersey, southeastern New York State including Long Island, and Massachusetts. It is also common in the upper Midwest, especially Wisconsin and Minnesota, and on the West Coast. Outside the United States Lyme disease occurs in Canada, northern Europe, Asia, and Australia.

Noticeable symptoms: After being in the woods or even in a backyard frequented by deer, you may find a very small tick attached to your skin and feeding on blood. In the spring the tick may be as small as the period at the end of this sentence. Many people do not even notice the tick bite. A tick bite does not mean that you will get Lyme disease, but it can alert you to watch for symptoms.

A characteristic *bull's-eye rash*, red with clearing at the center (see illustration) appears in perhaps three out of five infections. This rash usually lasts for two or three weeks. Often, however, there is no rash, and the first indication of disease is a series of flu-like symptoms, including fever, sore throat, fatigue, headache, and aching joints. Bell's palsy, affecting muscles in the face, may be a symptom.

Diagnosis: Lyme disease shares symptoms with many other illnesses, so one of the main tasks of the physician is to eliminate other possible causes. Lyme disease is suspected primarily in regions where it is common. If other diseases are ruled out, a doctor may take a blood sample and send it to a laboratory. Results may not be available from the sample for several days. In some cases the physician may choose to begin treatment before reviewing the results of the blood test. In a region where there is a high rate of Lyme disease, physicians sometimes prescribe antibiotics after a bite from a blacklegged tick or on the appearance of a bull's-eye rash.

Treatment options: Lyme disease can usually be cured by antibiotics. Early-stage treatment may consist of pills only or a combination of shots and pills. It is important to follow the doctor's directions on length of time to keep taking the medicine.

If not treated promptly, bacteria may hide in tissues and develop resistance. Hospitalization may be necessary to permit the use of very strong antibiotics.

Stages and progress: If untreated, the original flulike symptoms of Lyme disease disappear after a few weeks. A new set of symptoms, often including severe headaches, emerges. Often the disease settles in the joints, producing Lyme arthritis, a painful condition that persists indefinitely without treatment. Sometimes the disease causes tics, nerve damage, or mental problems. Patients often complain of fatigue. Some report personality changes, intolerance to noise, or depression. It is not known whether the disease can damage the unborn child of a pregnant woman. Lyme disease does not lead to death.

Phone doctor

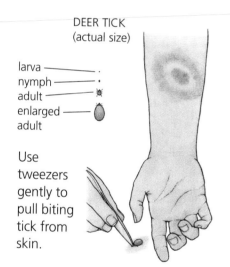

DEER TICK
(actual size)

larva ——— .
nymph ——— :
adult ——— ☀
enlarged ———
adult

Use tweezers gently to pull biting tick from skin.

Bull's-eye rash
A red region in the shape of a target or a doughnut forms around a tick bite at the start of many cases of Lyme disease. This bull's-eye rash is called *erythema migrans* by physicians.

Parents find a new disease

In the early 1970s parents and physicians in a part of Connecticut along Long Island Sound began to notice that children from the region developed a localized rash followed by fever, chills, and muscle aches. Some of the children also developed a form of arthritis.

One of the parents investigated the disease, and in 1975 Dr. Allen C. Steere described it to other doctors. He named it Lyme disease after the community of Old Lyme, Connecticut, where the ailment had first been noticed. Lyme disease was found in 1978 to be borne by the blacklegged tick *Ixodes scapularis;* the bacterium that causes the disease was identified in 1982 and later named *Borrelia burgdorferi.* Eventually, researchers recognized that Lyme disease is the same illness as one that had puzzled doctors in Scandinavia since the 1880s.

Prevention: In regions where Lyme disease occurs, dress to keep ticks from biting in bushy or wooded areas, including backyards. Wear a long-sleeved shirt, long pants tucked into the tops of socks, and a hat. Ticks cannot leap or fly, so you will not be bitten unless you brush against a place where a tick is waiting. Apply an insect repellent containing the ingredient DEET or the insecticide Duranon to your clothing. ***Do not use repellents or insecticides directly on your skin.*** On leaving the yard or woods, bathe or shower, and look carefully for ticks. Have someone remove with tweezers any tick you find. The longer the tick feeds—it could stay attached for hours or even days—the greater the chance of transmitting enough bacteria to cause the disease. Check all over your body for the bull's-eye rash every time you bathe. If the rash is spotted, or if flulike symptoms develop after possible exposure, visit your physician at the earliest opportunity.

Discouraging deer, white-footed mice, other rodents, and even (in the West) lizards from coming close to your house or commonly used yard areas can help. Keep grass mowed, and avoid plants that attract deer, such as yews. Clean up brush or other places where rodents can live or obtain food. Check pets frequently for ticks.

Various insecticides will kill ticks in a limited area, such as yards or gardens. These should be applied by professionals only.

Vaccines have been developed for Lyme disease, but these are not completely effective and have produced some serious adverse reactions. After several years of experience with the vaccine used in the United States, the manufacturer ceased to market it in 2002, citing poor sales as the cause.

Lymphatic system

BODY SYSTEM

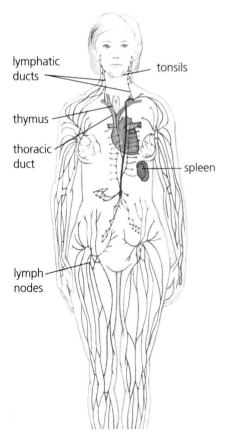

Lymphatic system

When blood passes through the capillaries, it loses some of its plasma, which joins a liquid found between cells known as *lymph* (LIHMF). Lymph must be returned to the circulatory system to keep blood volume fairly constant. Some liquid seeps back through capillary walls, but a system of tubes called the lymphatic system drains some 60% of lymph back into the blood.

Size and location: The lymphatic system is similar in many ways to the venous system. Small *lymph capillaries* collect lymph from between the cells. One-way valves keep lymph moving slowly along through larger *lymph vessels,* although lymph moves much more slowly than blood in the veins, where pumping of the heart pushes blood along. The lymph vessels grow larger and culminate in two *lymphatic ducts* that drain the lymph into large veins just behind the collarbone, letting the lymph rejoin the blood plasma.

Along the way lymph passes through masses of spongy tissue called *lymph nodes;* these filter out any debris, including bacteria, from the lymph. While there are lymph nodes wherever two lymph vessels are joined, they are thickest in the elbow, knee, armpit, and groin. The spleen is sometimes thought of as the largest of all lymph nodes, but it also has other roles. The thymus is another specialized lymph node, but the most famous lymph nodes are the *tonsils.* Lymph nodes are sometimes called lymph glands, although they are not glands in the modern sense of the word.

Role: Lymph nodes are made from *lymphoid tissue,* but they are not the only organs where lymphoid tissue is found; it is found everywhere that bacteria or other germs can easily invade the body, specifically in the linings of the parts of the body that are exposed to the outside, such as the respiratory system and parts of the digestive system. Much of the action of the immune system takes place in lymphoid tissue. Certain white blood cells, the agranular leukocytes, form in lymph nodes; other white blood cells are more common in lymph than they are in blood.

Phone doctor

The lymphatic system also transports some nutrients, especially fats, from the digestive system to the blood.

Conditions that affect the lymphatic system: Whenever lymph vessels become blocked, fluids cannot drain properly from cells. The fluids build up and produce the swelling called edema or lymphedema. Parasites that block the lymph vessels can cause massive edema, known as elephantiasis. Surgery to remove lymph nodes, a step often taken to treat cancers, can lead to lymphedema as well. The much smaller swelling of blisters and hives is caused by infection, injury, or allergic reaction blocking the flow of lymph.

Any disease that reduces the number of white blood cells or makes them abnormal and ineffective affects the lymphatic system. Cancers in white blood cells are relatively common. They are separated into Hodgkin's disease and *non-Hodgkin's lymphoma*. Hodgkin's disease is a cancer of the white blood cells called *macrophages*, while non-Hodgkin's lymphoma affects different white blood cells. Nonmalignant tumors at lymph nodes, also known as lymphomas, can occur as well.

Leukemias are different from lymphomas in that the site of production of the aberrant cells is the bone marrow or elsewhere instead of the lymph system. AIDS, caused by HIV infection of the white blood cells, produces a characteristic swelling of the lymph nodes along with abnormalities in white blood cells.

Infection of the lymph system, often with streptococci, causes symptoms that may be called blood poisoning, but properly are known as *lymphangitis* (LIHM-faan-JIY-tihs). Symptoms include fine red streaks radiating from a wound or bite. ***This condition is a serious threat to health and needs treatment by a physician.*** Antibiotics clear it up in most cases.

Lymphocytes

(LIHM-fuh-SIYTZ)

BODY SYSTEM

Although each red blood cell is almost exactly like every other, the cells we think of as white blood cells (formally known as *leukocytes*) come in at least a dozen different varieties with various roles in the immune system's defense of the body. Perhaps the best known of the white blood cells are the lymphocytes, which form about a quarter of all the white blood cells. Another large group is

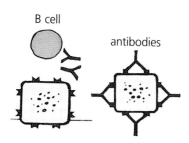

B cell

antibodies

Bacteria, other cells of all kinds, and viruses expose proteins on their membranes or coats. Antibodies produced by B cells are keys that lock into specific proteins and inactivate them. The result is that the cell or virus can no longer function.

the cell-devouring *phagocytes.* The remainder include *mast cells* and *granulocytes,* both largely involved in allergic reactions.

Size and location: Lymphocytes, like most cells, are microscopic. Under the microscope they can be seen to be about the same size as the red blood cells, but less regular in shape and, of course, not red. Although lymphocytes are known as white blood cells, more are found in the lymph than in blood. Draining all the lymph from an animal's body removes all the lymphocytes.

Some white blood cells are produced from stem cells in bone marrow along with red blood cells. Other lymphocytes are formed in the lymph nodes by cell division. The daughter cells from one lymphocyte form a *line* of lymphocytes that are all related to each other and that share particular characteristics.

Role: There are three types of lymphocytes. The *natural killer cells* are a generalized response to any type of foreign invader, but the other two develop quite specific responses.

The *T lymphocytes* are those that must mature in the thymus before they can be involved in the immune response (the "T" is for thymus). They are the principal cells involved in graft rejection, but they also have a role in fighting bacteria and other invaders, including cancer cells. Each line of T cells is trained to respond to a particular substance. The loss of one type of T cell is a major symptom of AIDS, although the HIV virus that causes AIDS seems to affect the immune system in many other ways as well.

The *B lymphocytes* mature outside the thymus in mammals. In birds B lymphocytes mature in an organ that humans do not have, the bursa of Fabricius (the "B" stands for bursa). B cells react to invaders by releasing chemicals called *antibodies.* An antibody is a chemical that is specific to a particular protein, sugar, nucleic acid, or fat, but the strongest reaction is with a protein. If, for example, a measles virus is in the blood or lymph, a B lymphocyte will release an antibody that attaches to a protein on the surface of the virus. One kind of T cell then stimulates the production of many B cells that release the same antibody. The next measles virus that comes along is met with great amounts of the antibody, causing immunity to measles.

Conditions that affect the lymphocytes: Infections of many kinds can produce too many or too few lymphocytes, but the number returns to normal when the infection is resolved. Lymphocyte cell lines that develop cancer produce *non-Hodgkin's lymphoma* or one of the lymphocytic leukemias. Infection of the T cells by the HIV virus is the cause of AIDS.

Lymphoma
(lihm-FOH-muh)

DISEASE

TYPE: CANCER

See also
Blood
Cancers
Hodgkin's disease
Immune system
Lymphatic system
Lymphocytes

Phone doctor

Cancers that develop in the lymph glands are called lymphomas. There are two general types: Hodgkin's disease (discussed elsewhere) and *non-Hodgkin's lymphoma* (discussed here).

Cause: Most cases of non-Hodgkin's lymphoma originate in the B lymphocytes, but the cause is unknown. One type, Burkitt's lymphoma, found primarily in Africa, is at least partly induced by exposure to the Epstein-Barr virus. The HIV virus that causes AIDS also appears to increase the risk of lymphoma. In some other cases suppression of the immune system plays a role; for example, people with organ transplants are at higher risk of lymphoma because of their altered immune function. Certain environments produce more cases, such as farms that use chemical pesticides and manufacturing sites that use benzene.

Incidence: Approximately 53,000 new cases of non-Hodgkin's lymphoma occurred annually in the United States in the late 1990s, but the rate has been steadily increasing and reached perhaps 70,000 cases by the early 2000s. Incidence increases with age, and the disease is more common in males than females.

Noticeable symptoms: Swollen lymph glands usually are the first indication of lymphoma. Other symptoms include itching, fever, night sweats, fatigue, and weight loss.

Diagnosis: A doctor will perform a biopsy of tissue from the lymph glands and nodes—remove tissue for examination under a microscope—to learn if cancerous cells are present and to distinguish non-Hodgkin's lymphoma from Hodgkin's disease. Other tests also may be performed, including x-rays, scans of the liver and spleen, and blood chemistry analyses.

Treatment options: Chemotherapy is usually effective, but if the disease is localized, radiation therapy is generally the treatment of choice. In later stages of the disease both radiation and chemotherapy may be used. Some patients with advanced lymphoma may benefit from bone-marrow transplants.

Stages and progress: Initially lymphoma involves a single organ or region of lymph nodes. As the disease progresses, additional areas of the body become involved. Without treatment the disease is fatal. With early treatment about half of the patients survive at least five years following diagnosis. Even in advanced cases treatment can often induce complete remission.

Macrophages

See **Phagocytes and other leukocytes**

Macular degeneration

DISEASE

TYPE: MECHANICAL

See also
Detached retina
Eyes and vision
Tobacco and disease

A painless disease of the eye, macular degeneration affects a small region in the center of the retina, the light-sensitive membrane at the back of the eyeball. This region, where the cells responsible for sharp color vision are located, is the *macula* (MAAK-yuh-luh). Macular degeneration results in progressive loss of central vision.

Cause: One form of macular degeneration occurs as cellular debris slowly builds up under the macula. But a faster developing form, called *wet macular degeneration,* occurs when tiny amounts of blood seep through capillaries into surrounding space, causing scar tissue to form. As a result the center of the retina separates from the underlying tissue of the eyeball. Sometimes the separation takes many months, but it can also happen in a matter of days. Macular degeneration differs from detached retina in that the edges of the retina stay in place. Without treatment the disease prevails, and even though peripheral vision remains, the stricken individual becomes legally blind.

Incidence and risk factors: Macular degeneration is common, affecting some 13 million in the United States, mostly senior citizens. After age 75 nearly one out of five experience it to some degree. Members of some families appear to be especially prone to the disease.

Noticeable symptoms: People with macular degeneration may first notice a tiny spot of fuzziness in the center of vision. Normally straight lines appear wavy; colors, instead of being clear and bright, become increasingly gray. The fuzzy spot grows over time until such activities as reading at a normal distance and driving a car become extremely difficult. Eventually, all that remains is peripheral vision—the ability to see out of the corners of the eyes. Macular degeneration generally, but not always, affects both eyes, but the condition may not become apparent until the second eye is affected.

Diagnosis: An ophthalmologist often can observe deposits under the macula, perhaps using a dye and photographing the region. But the principal test consists of having the patient stare at a grid with a dot in the middle; a person with macular degeneration can see the grid, which may have wavy lines, but the center dot is invisible.

Don't smoke

Prevention: There is no specific method for preventing macular degeneration from starting, although there is evidence that smoking induces it. Twice as many smokers develop the disease as nonsmokers.

People with intermediate or early macular degeneration may be able to slow the disease with high doses of antioxidant vitamins plus zinc. According to a study in 2001, this dietary approach even stopped the disease from developing in many cases. Vitamin and mineral supplements should be taken only under a physician's care, however, as the zinc can produce anemia. Later stages of one form of the disease can be slowed by laser treatments to stop the bleeding.

The ophthalmologist's printed grid with the center dot is sometimes given to people who have a high probability of developing the disease. They can perform the test on themselves at home on a daily basis. If the lines appear wavy or if they are indistinct in some areas, laser treatments are begun immediately.

A number of near-vision aids can help afflicted individuals to remain independent by maintaining their ability to navigate. These aids include high-intensity lighting and magnifying lenses.

Mad cow disease and CJD-v

DISEASE

TYPE: INFECTIOUS (PRION)

See also
Animal diseases and humans
Creutzfeldt-Jakob disease
Emerging diseases
Prions

During the 1980s Great Britain experienced an epidemic of *bovine spongiform encephalopathy* (ehn-SEHF-uh-LOP-uh-thee), popularly called mad cow disease. A few years later (in 1996) a new form, or variant, of Creutzfeldt-Jakob disease (CJD) known as CJD-v appeared in humans. Mad cow disease and CJD are similar disorders that destroy brain tissue. This led to the theory, generally regarded as confirmed, that CJD-v is the human form of mad cow disease. The disease is fatal and has no known cure.

Parts affected: CJD-v and mad cow disease belong to a group of chronic wasting diseases called spongiform encephalopathies. These diseases produce spongelike holes in the brain and other nervous tissue.

Cause: CJD-v and mad cow disease appear to be caused by misfolded forms of proteins called prions. Evidence suggests that CJD-v is contracted by eating contaminated beef from cattle infected with mad cow disease. The abnormal cattle prions apparently prompt the patient's prions to twist into abnormal forms. It is possible that CJD-v can be transmitted from one human to another through organ donations, contaminated blood, or contaminated surgical instruments. It appears that people who develop CJD-v have a genetic trait that makes them susceptible to it.

Incidence: CJD-v affects younger patients than other types of CJD. It also causes damage that can be distinguished from other types of CJD. By 2001 CJD-v had claimed over a hundred lives, mostly in the United Kingdom, but a few in other European countries as well. Mad cow disease has never been diagnosed in the United States, and there is no evidence that American cattle have ever caused the disease in humans.

Noticeable symptoms: The earliest symptoms of CJD-v are personality changes, including severe mood swings and depression. As the disease progresses, the victim may go blind and lose the ability to speak. Dementia develops and, shortly before death, a coma.

Diagnosis: A physician will look for psychiatric symptoms and ask about the patient's possible exposure to contaminated beef. If tests such as brain scans rule out other diseases, a brain biopsy will be performed to look for abnormal prions.

Stages and progress: CJD-v appears to have a long incubation period. People may be infected for years before symptoms appear. However, once symptoms are present, the disease progresses swiftly toward dementia and death. Most patients die within a year of diagnosis.

Prevention and risk factors: Cattle are believed to contract mad cow disease from protein feed supplements. In Britain until 1988 these supplements were made from brains and other offal from sheep, including sheep that had died of scrapie, a spongiform encephalopathy. Western countries have now taken stringent steps to stop this practice. Since 1989 the United States has banned imports of cattle and beef from countries with mad cow disease. Additional controls on the food supply were imposed after the first cases of CJD-v in 1996.

A similar encephalopathy in North American deer and elk, known as chronic wasting disease, is not known to have been transmitted to humans, but some researchers recommend that hunters of deer and elk be very careful to avoid consuming meat that includes any part of the brain or spinal column.

Malaria

DISEASE

TYPE: MOSQUITO-BORNE PARASITIC

People who travel to tropical parts of the world can get malaria. With proper precautions this serious disease can be prevented and most cases of it cured.

Cause: A bite from a female *Anopheles* (uh-NOF-uh-LEEZ) mosquito can spread malaria. Within the salivary glands of the mosquito are the tiny microorganisms that cause the disease. These microscopic parasites belong to one of four species of *Plasmodium* (plaaz-MOH-dee-uhm), a type of one-celled protist. When the mosquito pierces human skin to take a meal of blood, some of the parasites enter the body, travel to the liver, and then migrate into the bloodstream, where they reproduce.

Incidence: Malaria is a tropical disease found primarily in the equatorial regions of South and Central America, Africa, and Asia. However, instances of the disease are found in Europe and North America among people who have traveled to tropical regions. In 1999 about 12,000 such travelers were infected.

The complex life cycle of the malaria parasite begins when certain merozoites released by burst red blood cells reach a mosquito's stomach, where they mature into sexual forms and mate. Sexual reproduction in the mosquito is followed by the first asexual stage, the sporozoites, which migrate into the salivary glands of the mosquito and await injection into a suitable bird or mammal.

In a human the sporozoites reproduce asexually in the liver, forming the first generation of merozoites. These reproduce asexually in red blood cells as second-generation merozoites, some of which eventually become the sexual forms.

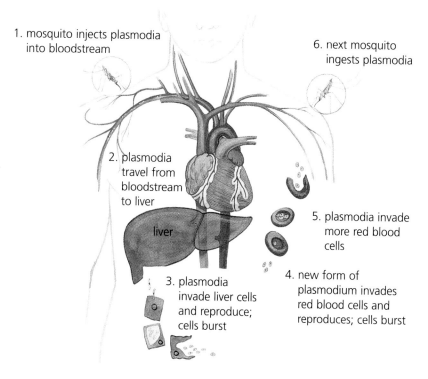

1. mosquito injects plasmodia into bloodstream

6. next mosquito ingests plasmodia

2. plasmodia travel from bloodstream to liver

liver

5. plasmodia invade more red blood cells

3. plasmodia invade liver cells and reproduce; cells burst

4. new form of plasmodium invades red blood cells and reproduces; cells burst

Phone doctor

Worldwide it is the most serious human disease, with from 400 million to 900 million new cases reported each year. Estimates for the number of people killed annually range from 700,000 to 2.7 million, including one child every 30 seconds.

Noticeable symptoms: The symptoms characteristic of malaria are chills, fever, shaking, profuse sweating, and fatigue. These symptoms come and go in regular waves, timed with the reproductive cycle of the parasites. In some instances urine may be dark colored. ***Anyone who has been in a region known to harbor malaria should see a doctor at the first sign of any of these symptoms.***

Diagnosis: Blood tests reveal that a person with malaria has anemia, a reduction in the number of red blood cells. This condition is caused by the destruction of red blood cells as the malaria-causing parasites reproduce. The job of the red blood cells is to carry oxygen to each cell. Without enough oxygen cell respiration is reduced, leaving the victim tired and lacking in energy. Parasites can also be detected in the red blood cells. In addition, a person with malaria develops an enlarged spleen, the organ that normally removes damaged blood cells from blood.

Treatment options: To treat malaria people are given the drug *chloroquine* in pill form or by injection into muscle to kill the parasites in the bloodstream. If the parasites are resistant to this treatment, a combination of quinine, pyrimethamine, and antibiotics is used.

Stages and progress: After the initial bite that introduces the parasite into the bloodstream, the stages and progress of the disease differ depending on which *Plasmodium* species has infected the body. Each has a slightly different life cycle, causing a difference in the length and severity of bouts of chills and fever (see illustration). The most common form of the disease is *tertian* (TUR-shuhn) *malaria,* usually caused by *Plasmodium vivax.* Typically, the chills, fever, and profuse sweating occur every 48 hours. *Plasmodium ovale* causes a milder case of malaria characterized by only a few short attacks. Another organism, *Plasmodium malariae,* causes *quartan* (KWORT-uhn) *malaria.* Rather than every 48 hours, the attacks come at intervals of 72 hours.

The most severe form is *falciparum* (faal-SIHP-uh-ruhm) *malaria,* caused by the *Plasmodium falciparum* protozoa. This form of malaria often infects the brain as well as the blood. If caught early, a person with falciparum malaria can be treated and recover completely. If not, the disease can progress and be fatal. Anemia and loss of fluids (dehydration) may cause death. If falciparum malaria becomes chronic, it can cause *blackwater fever,* a condition of the liver and kidneys in which the patient bleeds internally, passing dark-colored urine.

Prevention: Swampy regions where mosquitoes breed are the most likely places to catch malaria. Throughout the world swamps have been drained and insecticides used to destroy mosquito populations, reducing the incidence of malaria. Over several decades of spraying pesticides, however, some mosquitoes have developed resistance to the pesticides that were sprayed the most. This has made eradicating the disease much more difficult.

When visiting or living in an area where malaria occurs, certain precautions should be taken. Antimalarial drugs can be administered in advance and taken daily to prevent its occur-

Barking up the right tree: the rain forest cure for malaria

During the Age of Exploration, when Europeans first ventured into South America, many were bitten by infected mosquitoes and developed malaria. The explorers were treated by the indigenous people, who used bark from certain trees to alleviate the symptoms of the disease. The Europeans named the trees *cinchona,* after the Countess of Chinchon, the wife of a seventeenth-century viceroy from Peru who was treated with the bark.

Cinchona trees are tropical members of the madder family. The active ingredient in their bark is *quinine,* a word derived from the native Peruvian name for the tree bark extract. Quinine and its related chemicals are effective for treating malaria and reducing fever. These alkaloid drugs have a characteristic bitter taste and are now synthesized in a laboratory rather than made from bark.

rence. Mosquito repellent should be applied to the skin and mosquito netting used in sleeping quarters to prevent the bite of an infected mosquito.

Although scientists have worked on developing a vaccine against malaria, none has proven useful so far. This is because as the parasite goes through its different life stages, it changes the chemical makeup of its cell coat. A vaccine with antibodies to fight one stage of the organism cannot fight another stage because the protein coat of each stage is different.

Sickle cell trait offers protection from malaria

Many Africans and African Americans carry the genetic trait for sickle cell anemia. In parts of tropical Africa a large percentage of the population carries the trait. This would seem quite unusual given that getting the trait from both parents usually causes a fatal blood disease. But having just one copy of the trait seems to lower a person's chances of getting malaria. Although a person who inherits the trait from one parent does not get sickle cell disease, some of the red blood cells do show the sickle cell characteristic. In 1953 scientists first noticed that the trait for sickle cell anemia seemed to occur more frequently in places where there was a high incidence of falciparum malaria. How could the two facts be related?

"Sickled" red blood cells have irregular, crescent shapes rather than round shapes. They are also rigid and tend to block blood vessels, causing anemia. However, if a red blood cell is infected with a malaria parasite, the cell sickles more readily, then dies, killing the parasite inside it before it can reproduce. The body's immune cells have a better chance of getting rid of the remaining disease-causing organisms before a full-blown case of malaria develops. So in tropical locations sickled blood cells actually provide a defense against malaria.

Mal du mer	*See* **Seasickness**
Malignancies	*See* **Cancers**
Manic depressive syndrome	*See* **Bipolar disorder**

Marfan syndrome
(MAHR-faan)

DISEASE

TYPE: GENETIC

See also
Aneurysm
Arteries
Circulatory system
Detached retina
Eyes and vision
Fractures, dislocations, sprains, and strains
Genetic diseases
Heart
Scoliosis

People who are affected by Marfan syndrome have a defect in one of the proteins that are the main building blocks of cells. The protein, called *fibrillin* (FIY-brih-lihn), is especially abundant in connective tissue, the tissue that gives substance and support to bones, tendons and ligaments, cartilage, blood vessels, and heart valves. When fibrillin is scarce or its structure is faulty, a wide variety of signs and symptoms may appear, ranging from changes in outward appearance to defects in such organs as the eyes and heart.

Cause: The gene responsible for the formation of fibrillin lies on chromosome 15. Marfan syndrome can apparently result from any one of a large number of possible mutations in the gene. The wide range of these mutations may account for the wide range of physical effects that the condition produces.

Marfan syndrome is a dominant condition (see Genetic diseases). It is most often inherited from an affected parent. About a quarter of all cases, however, appear to result from some new mutation, either in the father's sperm or the mother's egg. Moreover, a mildly affected parent can have a severely affected child, a severely affected parent can have a mildly affected child, brothers and sisters can be affected to different degrees, and so forth.

Incidence: Marfan syndrome is believed to affect about 1 in 5,000 people in the United States. That figure may be low, since some of those who have the condition have never been diagnosed with it.

Noticeable symptoms: The observable signs of Marfan syndrome vary widely. They are seldom apparent at birth, and they may not become recognizable until adolescence or adulthood, if then. Sometimes they are so mild that they go completely unnoticed.

The most visible effects are those that involve the bones and joints. A person with Marfan syndrome tends to be unusually tall, with long arms and legs and "spidery" fingers. The face may be narrow, with a high-arched palate (roof of the mouth) and crowded teeth. The joints are likely to be exceptionally loose, particularly in the hands and wrists, and dislocation of joints is common. The spine may be twisted out of line (scoliosis), and the breastbone may either bulge forward or form a sunken valley between the ribs.

The eyes are often affected. The lens of the eye is held in place by ligaments. Fibrillin deficiency may weaken these ligaments so that the lens slips off center, a condition called *ectopia lentis* (ehk-TOH-pee-uh LEHN-tihs), "displacement of the lens." The defect makes vision less sharp but does not cause blindness. Regardless of whether lenses are displaced, nearsightedness (myopia) is common, and detached retina occurs more often than in the general population.

More common and potentially more serious are effects on the heart valves, which normally keep blood flowing in a single direction through the heart. One or more of the valves may not close properly, so that some blood leaks backward rather than moving forward. The heart must then work harder to make up for the diminished flow; it tends to become enlarged, with a risk of eventual failure.

Most dangerous of all is weakening of the body's largest artery, the aorta. Blood is pumped at high pressure through the part of the aorta where it leaves the heart. When the aorta's walls just above the heart are weakened by fibrillin deficiency, they bulge outward, forming an aneurysm. Tears in the stretched walls may cause blood to leak between the layers, and a sudden, large split can cause death from massive internal bleeding.

Diagnosis: Outward signs of Marfan syndrome, such as skeletal changes or vision blurred by displaced lenses, are generally less useful for diagnosis than internal signs such as a faulty heart valve or a weakened aorta. Blood leaking backward through a valve defect, for example, may cause a heart murmur, audible through a stethoscope.

Family history can be a useful tool in diagnosis. If one or more family members are known to be affected, a child may be carefully and repeatedly examined for the telltale signs of the condition.

Because the gene for fibrillin is subject to so many different mutations, neither DNA analysis nor other genetic testing offers a simple way to identify affected individuals. Sometimes analysis of DNA in families with affected members can isolate the mutation that produces the syndrome in that specific group.

Treatment options: Early treatment can help head off at least some of the harmful effects of the disorder. Physical therapy, a supportive brace, or surgery can be used to correct spinal deformation. Orthodontics can widen the jaw and allow more room for crowded teeth. Glasses can improve weakened vision.

But the most important forms of treatment are intended to minimize the risks of heart and aorta damage. Individuals with the disorder are advised to avoid strenuous exercise and heavy exertion, which raise the blood pressure. They may also take medicines to reduce blood pressure. Since their heart valves are especially susceptible to infections, they are given preventive antibiotics whenever they undergo any medical treatment (including dental treatment) that might penetrate blood vessels. In severe cases surgery may be needed to repair or replace a faulty heart valve. When the aorta is greatly enlarged, a synthetic tube may be surgically inserted to replace the damaged section.

Mastitis
(maa-STIY-tihs)

DISEASE

TYPE: INFECTIOUS (BACTERIAL)

Mastitis is an inflammation of breast tissue. It usually occurs in mothers who are breastfeeding their infants. However, it can occur in women who are neither pregnant nor breastfeeding. It also can occur in newborn babies.

Incidence: About 1 in 20 nursing mothers develop mastitis. It can develop at any time during breastfeeding, but it is most common 10 to 28 days following birth of the baby. It generally does not affect both breasts at the same time.

See also
Bacteria and disease
Fever

Phone doctor

Cause: Mastitis is a bacterial infection. It usually develops when bacteria pass from the baby's mouth or nose into the mother's breast through the nipple. This is most likely to occur if there is a crack or sore in the nipple.

Noticeable symptoms: The infected breast may feel sore and become red and swollen. The woman may develop a fever, chills, and other flulike symptoms. If these symptoms persist for more than 24 hours, if blood or pus is present in the milk, or if fever becomes high, the woman should see her doctor or midwife.

Meanwhile, the woman should continue to breastfeed her baby unless it is too painful to do so. Frequent nursing keeps the milk supply flowing and prevents blocking of the milk ducts. This provides relief of symptoms and clears up the infection faster. There is no danger to the baby: Antibodies in the mother's milk protect the baby from the bacteria.

Relief of symptoms: In addition to frequent breastfeeding, the application of moist heat may relieve pain. For example, the woman might apply a hot-water bottle to her breasts or soak her breasts in warm water several times a day. She also should rest, drink plenty of fluids, and avoid pressure on the breast, such as that caused by a tight bra.

If symptoms continue for more than 24 hours, the health-care worker will prescribe an antibiotic to combat the bacteria. Diagnosed early, mastitis is easy to treat; but if left untreated, an abscess may develop, requiring surgery.

Prevention: Stress, fatigue, and poor diet increase susceptibility to infection. Nursing mothers are advised to get plenty of rest and eat a healthy, balanced diet.

Measles (rubeola)

DISEASE

TYPE: INFECTIOUS (VIRAL)

The word *measle* in an early form of English meant "blemish." The disease measles, characterized by spots on the skin, has gone by many different names: red measles, hard measles, and nine-day measles; physicians call it *rubeola*. About 900 A.D. the Arabic scholar Rhazes recognized measles as a separate disease. It is not the same as "German" measles, or rubella.

Cause: Measles is a very contagious disease caused by a virus. The measles virus is passed from person to person by exhaled droplets from the nose and throat.

Incidence: Prior to 1963, when the first measles vaccine became available, large outbreaks occurred almost every year. Sometimes so many children were ill that elementary schools were closed until the outbreak was over. Until the 1960s about 90% of the population had measles by the age of 20. The development of a vaccination for measles and requirements that children be vaccinated before entering school have dramatically reduced the incidence. In 2000 there were only 152 reported cases of measles in the United States.

Noticeable symptoms: Measles begins with a fever, cough, and runny nose. This is followed in a few days by a rash of small, slightly raised spots. The rash usually begins on the head and face and moves down the body.

Diagnosis: Measles is now so rare in the United States that physicians may not suspect it at first. One characteristic sets it apart from other rashes, however. Small patches of infection inside the mouth (called Koplik's spots) are not seen in similar rashes with a different cause. A doctor can do a blood test to identify measles, but usually this is not necessary.

Treatment options: Like most diseases caused by viruses, measles must run its course—that is, although it cannot be cured by medications, the immune system will eventually overpower it. Bed rest and keeping the patient comfortable are the most effective treatments. Some individuals become sensitive to light and are more comfortable in a darkened room. Some benefit from a humidifier because it makes it easier for them to breathe. Sinus pills, which combine acetaminophen with a decongestant, also help relieve symptoms.

Stages and progress: The first symptoms of measles occur ten to twelve days after infection. During the initial period of fever, runny nose, and cough the patient feels miserable. On the third or fourth day the fever drops, and tiny white spots appear on the inside of the mouth. Next the fever returns, and the itchy rash begins. The rash spreads, the red spots on the skin get larger and run together. After four to seven days the rash begins to disappear; it is gone in a day or two.

Most cases of measles, especially those in children, are uncomplicated. Children under 5 years of age and adults over 20 have more severe cases and are more likely to experience complications. One reason is that the measles virus invades the immune system and reduces protection against other diseases. The most common complications are diarrhea (8%), middle ear infections, or otitis media (7%), and pneumonia (6%); but inflammation of the brain, or encephalitis (0.1%), and convulsions can also occur. Because of the possibility of complications, which sometimes, but rarely, can be fatal, measles should never be taken lightly.

Emergency Room

The danger of complications can be reduced by good observation of symptoms. Talk with a doctor if the sick individual complains of earaches or headaches, or if the symptoms linger for more than a week after the rash appears. *If convulsions occur, get medical help immediately.*

Prevention and risk factors: A person infected with measles virus can transmit it to others from about five days before symptoms appear to about five days after they appear. Because measles is very contagious, it is difficult to prevent exposure.

Get vaccinated

The best prevention for measles is vaccination. The MMR is a vaccine to prevent measles, mumps, and rubella; it is given in two doses. The first dose is given when a child is 12 to 15 months old; the second is given when a child is 4 to 6 years old in preparation for entering school. Most people born before January 1, 1957, have had measles and have natural immunity to the disease. Anyone born after that date needs two doses of MMR vaccine at least four weeks apart to protect them from measles.

"German" measles (rubella), caused by a different virus, can pose serious risks to the developing fetus of a pregnant woman. Measles (rubeola) does not carry the same risk, but can result in premature labor, spontaneous abortion, and low-birthweight babies. If a pregnant woman is immunized, she is probably safe in settings where measles might be spread, but she should discuss this with her doctor. If an unvaccinated woman is pregnant, she is advised to delay vaccination until after pregnancy.

Melanoma

(MEHL-uh-NOH-muh)

DISEASE

TYPE: CANCER

Phone doctor

Melanoma ranks as the most dangerous of all skin cancers. However, when treatment begins before the cancer becomes well established, doctors can cure most cases. This makes early detection of melanoma especially important. About 30% of all melanomas first appear in an existing mole. *Do not hesitate to contact your doctor if you have a mole that suddenly changes color or size or becomes irregular in shape.*

Cause: Melanoma gets its name because it occurs in the pigment-producing cells, or melanocytes, in skin. Doctors believe that damage from ultraviolet radiation in sunlight is the chief cause of melanoma. Sunburn from this higher-energy light can damage DNA in melanocytes, causing cancer years later. Other possible causes include exposure to x-rays or chemical pollution. Heredity is also a factor. Some families tend to have moles that become cancerous. Different ethnic groups have differing susceptibilities.

Incidence: Medical experts report melanoma is on the increase, the number of cases having doubled in the United States over the past two decades. More than 50,000 persons develop melanoma each year, and about 7,000 die from the cancer. The risk of melanoma over a person's lifetime is 15 times as high for European Americans as for African Americans.

Noticeable symptoms: Generally, be suspicious of any mole that suddenly changes size, becomes irregular in shape, swells up or bleeds, itches, or becomes painful. *Consult your doctor as soon as possible after you notice any such symptoms connected with a mole.* The changes to look for in an existing mole or in the appearance of a new mole have been called the ABCDs of melanoma: Asymmetry of the mole, Border irregularity, Color (brown, blue, or black), and Diameter greater than that of a pencil. However, different varieties of melanoma have somewhat different appearances.

Superficial spreading melanoma starts as a small, fast-growing, irregularly shaped patch on the skin. The patch may range from flesh colored to black and could be spotted with other colors, including blue, red, purple, and white.

Nodular melanoma appears as a small, shiny bump or

growth that is firm to the touch. It usually ranges from pearl white to black in color. The growth may begin bleeding and then not heal completely. This type usually develops when people are between the ages of 20 and 60.

Choroid melanoma forms on the choroid tissue of the eye, just behind the retina. It is usually discovered during an eye examination before there are any symptoms, although if it is distorting the retina, it will produce vision problems. Although rare, this is the most common cancer of the eye in adults. It usually develops in older persons.

Diagnosis: The shape and colors of a suspected growth will probably be enough for your doctor to visually diagnose it as a melanoma. But a skin biopsy will be necessary to confirm that it is in fact cancerous. Depending on how advanced the melanoma is, your doctor may decide that further testing is needed to determine whether the cancer has spread. This could include a complete physical examination and even a CT scan to look for places where the cancer may have spread to other organs.

Treatment options: The accepted way to treat any melanoma is to remove it surgically, along with a margin of healthy skin around it. The larger the melanoma, the larger the margin of healthy skin that must be removed, to ensure against the chance that cancerous cells have spread. The surgeon may perform a skin graft to cover the site where the melanoma was removed to promote healing. If the melanoma has spread to nearby lymph nodes, these probably will also have to be removed.

Depending on the stage of the melanoma, further postoperative treatment, including anticancer drugs, may be called for. Follow-up examinations on a regular basis are necessary because the cancer may reappear. When melanomas are detected and treated early, treatment is successful in about 85% of cases.

Stages and progress: Though melanomas often do get started in an existing mole, about 70% of them appear in otherwise normal skin. The cancer begins in the skin's pigment-producing cells and at first spreads into the surrounding skin. The melanoma then enters a more dangerous stage, in which the growth thickens and spreads downward. Once it reaches the lymph system or circulatory system, the melanoma spreads to other parts of the body and becomes very difficult to cure. Without medical treatment melanoma is fatal.

Prevention and risk factors: Avoiding excessive exposure to sunlight, especially if you have light-colored skin, is the best way to prevent melanomas. Use commercially available lotions that block ultraviolet rays when you plan to be out in the sun. Wearing a hat with a broad brim also protects your face and neck from overexposure to the sun. Regularly examine your skin for suspicious growths or changes in existing moles, even in areas not exposed to the sun.

Stay out of sun

People with light-colored skin, red or blond hair, or blue eyes tend to be more susceptible to this form of cancer. People with dark-colored skin are less likely to get melanomas.

Meniere's disease

(MAYN-ee-uhrz)

DISEASE

TYPE: UNKNOWN

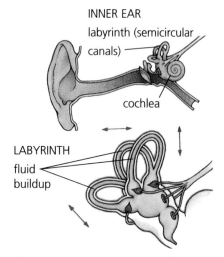

INNER EAR
labyrinth (semicircular canals)

cochlea

LABYRINTH
fluid buildup

Pressure buildup from fluids in the labyrinth of the inner ear causes the problems with balance and hearing that characterize Meniere's disease.

Meniere's disease, also known as *endolymphatic hydrops,* is a disorder of the inner ear that sometimes leads to permanent deafness. The disease brings on attacks of vertigo (dizziness), nausea, loss of balance, persistent ringing in the ears, and distorted hearing. Attacks come and go, lasting anywhere from a few minutes to hours at a time. Symptoms then disappear for hours, months, or even years. Hearing loss in the affected ear becomes progressively worse over a period of years.

The disease was first described in 1861 by French physician Prosper Ménière.

Cause: Meniere's disease occurs because something increases the pressure of fluids filling part of the inner ear called the *labyrinth.* One ear is usually affected when symptoms first appear, but anywhere from a quarter to a half of all patients eventually develop the condition in the other ear as well. Doctors do not know what causes most cases. The syndrome sometimes develops after a middle ear infection (otitis media), a blow to the head, an allergic attack, or syphilis.

Incidence: The disease usually strikes persons between 20 and 50 years of age.

Phone doctor

See also
Balance
Deafness
Dizziness
Nausea
Syphilis
Tinnitus

Avoid alcohol

No caffeine

Avoid salt

Practice meditation

Noticeable symptoms: Though the severity of symptoms may vary, most people with this disorder will eventually suffer attacks of vertigo serious enough to cause nausea, vomiting, and profuse sweating. There may be a sensation of pressure in the ears and usually a persistent ringing or buzzing in the ears. Muffled hearing or complete hearing loss in certain frequencies may accompany other symptoms.

Anyone suffering these symptoms for the first time should contact a physician as soon as possible. Unless told to do otherwise, it may be best to lie down and remain as still as possible until vertigo subsides.

Diagnosis: A doctor will probably conduct tests to determine the frequencies that are hard to hear and the extent of hearing loss. The specific test for Meniere's disease is designed to assess the balancing function of the inner ear. When water of different temperatures is inserted into the inner ear, people with Meniere's disease show an abnormal reaction, observable in the way the eyes flicker.

Treatment options: Medications can help relieve symptoms of dizziness and nausea as well as the anxiety that can accompany a severe attack. The physician may also recommend changes in diet, such as avoiding alcohol, cutting back on caffeine, and switching to low-salt foods to help reduce fluid retention. It is a good idea to avoid driving or even walking when visibility is low, since a person with Meniere's disease often depends on visual clues to maintain balance. Stress relief is sometimes helpful.

Surgery to relieve fluid pressure within the inner ear is an option when attacks are severe and other treatments fail. The surgeon may also decide that it is necessary to cut the nerve associated with the balance function.

Stages and progress: Meniere's disease usually begins with attacks in one ear but later affects the other in anywhere from a quarter to a half of the cases. The attacks of dizziness and nausea come and go with varying degrees of frequency and severity. There is a gradual loss of hearing in the affected ear over a period of a few years, but the symptoms sometimes disappear before it becomes complete.

Meningitis

(MEHN-ihn-JIY-tihs)

An infant suddenly develops a raging fever and has trouble breathing. The parents rush the baby to a hospital because they suspect the disease meningitis. Or, parents of teenagers or college students suddenly learn that a student at the school their child attends has experienced a case of meningitis and that all the students must be vaccinated.

Cause: Meningitis is an infectious disease caused by a variety of microorganisms, including several kinds of bacteria, viruses, and fungi. The disease-causing organisms can spread from person to person by droplets in the air.

Meningitis occurs as a result of an infection somewhere in the body such as in the sinuses or mastoids (cavities around the ear). The disease-causing organisms travel through the bloodstream to the *meninges* (muh-NIHN-jeez), the protective membranes that line the spinal cord and the brain. The attack on the meninges is nearly always a more serious infection than the original source, and when not treated is fatal.

Incidence: In the United States *bacterial meningitis* affects about 2,000 to 5,000 young people each year, 70% under the age of five. Although the typical older victim of meningitis is a teenager, there are also circumstances that bring higher risk. In adults bacterial meningitis occurs with higher frequency in alcoholics. Meningitis is also associated with the spread of some kinds of cancer and occurs more frequently in people whose immune system has been damaged by chemotherapy or AIDS. One type of bacterial meningitis, *tuberculous meningitis,* affects young children who live in regions where tuberculosis of the lungs is common.

Viral meningitis is far less serious than meningitis caused by bacteria or funguses. The disease may clear up in a week or two on its own. Viral meningitis occurs most often in winter, affecting 9,000 to 12,000 young people in the United States yearly.

Noticeable symptoms: In older children and adults the first symptoms may be severe headache, stiffness of the neck and upper back, and mental confusion, followed by fever, vomiting, skin rash, and then convulsions leading to loss of conscious-

Emergency Room

Phone doctor

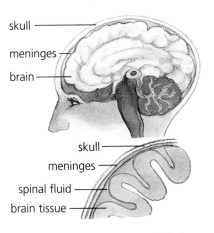

skull
meninges
brain

skull
meninges
spinal fluid
brain tissue

The meninges are layers of lining that help protect the brain and spinal column. But if they become inflamed and swell from an infection, they can cause serious damage to the central nervous system.

ness. *Anyone experiencing these serious symptoms should immediately seek medical help.*

In young children fever, vomiting, restlessness, and decreased levels of energy may be signs. Infants may develop symptoms very quickly and have a fever, diarrhea, difficult breathing, and uncontrolled convulsions. They may also show a yellowing of the skin called jaundice and a bulging of the soft spot in the skull. *These symptoms also call for immediate medical help.*

Diagnosis: A physician can test for meningitis by taking a *spinal tap,* a sample of spinal fluid drawn from the lumbar region of the spine. The blood from the fluid is tested, and a culture is made to reveal the identity of the disease-causing organism.

Treatment options: A diagnosis of bacterial meningitis requires immediate treatment with antibiotics, usually given intravenously in a hospital. Early detection and prompt treatment are crucial and can make the difference between full recovery and severe illness or even death. Mild cases of viral meningitis do not require hospitalization but should be treated with bed rest and any prescribed medications.

Stages and progress: Meningitis may come on quickly or gradually depending on the cause. Bacterial meningitis begins suddenly and progresses rapidly if untreated. It is fatal in about 15% of cases in adults, but significantly more deadly in infants and adults over 60. Before the days of antibiotics meningitis was more likely to be fatal; it left survivors blind, deaf, or mentally retarded. Even today with antibiotics, some people who recover suffer some permanent brain damage.

Prevention: Vaccination of children against *Hemophilus influenzae* has reduced the incidence of bacterial meningitis. Because of the variety of disease organisms other vaccines against meningitis are of limited use. They offer protection for only a short time and so are usually confined to localized outbreaks or to persons at greater risk because of other health conditions. Preventive doses of antibiotics are sometimes given to those in close contact with someone who has developed meningitis. To prevent infection, avoid contact with anyone with the disease.

Menstrual pain

SYMPTOM

Menstrual pain consists of the abdominal cramplike aching (with possible nausea, headache, backache, weakness, irritability, and depression) that accompanies the monthly intervals of menstruation in a woman. Its scientific name is *dysmenorrhea* (dihs-MEHN-uh-REE-uh). *Primary dysmenorrhea* results from excess effects of normal menstruation. *Secondary dysmenorrhea* is caused by disease or other malfunction.

Cause: The exact cause of menstrual pain remains unknown. The primary type is thought to result mainly from contractions of the uterus similar to but weaker than those that occur during childbirth. Such contractions are triggered by prostaglandins (PROS-tuh-GLAAN-dihnz), hormonelike chemicals that induce some effects of menstruation. It is believed that either production of prostaglandins or sensitivity to them varies and that such variation may explain why severity of menstrual pain differs among women.

Secondary dysmenorrhea appears during the menstrual cycle, but it is caused in most cases by infection, inflammation, or another disorder of the woman's reproductive organs.

Incidence: Half to three-quarters of all young women are subject to menstrual pain. Pain may be slight, but for about one woman in twenty it is severe enough to require cutting back on regular activities to some extent. Typically, women start experiencing menstrual pain in the early teenage years, about two years or more after their periods begin. Regular recurrence may begin when the cycle of ovulation becomes well established. It may lessen spontaneously starting in about the mid twenties.

Cases of secondary dysmenorrhea are comparatively uncommon.

Noticeable symptoms: Many women who get only mild onslaughts of primary dysmenorrhea typically feel headachy and have a tinge of nausea with vague discomfort and a sense of overfullness of the abdomen. Other women go through moderate to severe attacks. Symptoms of these may include cramping pain in the abdomen that varies from noticeable to very sharp; aching in the lower back; upset stomach with vomiting; headache; diarrhea; faintness; and emotional depression. These reactions generally start right before or with menstruation and dissipate in the first day or two of menstruation.

Secondary dysmenorrhea typically differs in duration. It tends to start a few days before menstruation and continues all through menstruation. Its characteristic major symptom is a not very sharp but heavy ache that feels lodged far down in the abdomen.

Diagnosis: In cases of secondary dysmenorrhea doctors look for evidence of a disorder of the reproductive organs or other organs in the pelvic area, such as endometriosis, PID (pelvic inflammatory disease), cysts, or benign tumor. An intrauterine device (IUD) used as a contraceptive may also lead to secondary dysmenorrhea.

Treatment: At least some relief of menstrual pain can be realized by reducing stress, exertion, and irritation. Helpful measures include getting increased rest, exercising in moderation, and putting a heating pad or hot-water bottle on the stomach. Common pain relievers such as ibuprofen (Motrin is a common trade name) are helpful, although sometimes prescription-strength doses are needed. Difficult cases of primary dysmenorrhea are nearly always relieved by prescription medicines that inhibit the production of prostaglandins.

Treatment of secondary dysmenorrhea often requires the help of a specialist to diagnose and correct the disorder that is its specific contributing cause.

Prevention: Attacks of menstrual pain tend to be heightened in their intensity when a woman is unusually fatigued or stressed. Making efforts to be as well rested and stress free as possible by the expected time of menstruation may reduce the severity.

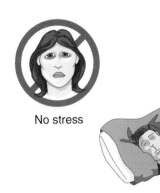

No stress

Rest

Oral contraceptives (birth-control pills) suppress ovulation and menstruation. Taking them therefore leaves a woman free of menstrual pain while they are active in her system.

Mental illnesses

Mental illnesses range from mild conditions such as fear of flying to incapacitating diseases that totally distort a person's perception of reality. Specialists in treating mental illnesses include *psychiatrists* (sih-KIY-uh-trihsts), who are medical doctors, and *psychologists* (siy-KOL-uh-jihsts), who have Ph.D.s but are not medical doctors. *Psychotherapist* is a general term for anyone who treats mental illness whether or not the therapist has specialized training.

Cause: People in the past attributed mental illness to possession by demons or other evil spirits. In recent years physicians have learned that for the most serious mental illnesses, termed *psychoses* (siy-KOH-seez—*psycho-* means "mind"), the demons are most often chemical in nature, although there may also be genetic and environmental factors.

Early in the nineteenth century physicians generally assumed that mental illness resulted from disease of the brain. This concept lost favor when—except for a few known disorders such as syphilis and lead poisoning—specific evidence was lacking. Also, near the end of the century therapies in which patients and doctors simply talked, such as *psychoanalysis* (SIY-koh-uh-NAAL-ih-sihs), a technique based on theories of Sigmund Freud, began to show some success. At that time few believed that talking alone could cure a physical condition. Thus, by the mid-twentieth century most psychiatrists rejected the idea of a physical basis for most mental illnesses.

Since then, however, common mental problems, especially serious mental illnesses, have been traced to chemical imbalances in the brain, perhaps with a genetic basis in some instances. Researchers have learned that talking by itself *can* change brain chemistry. Drugs that change the levels of chemicals in the brain also relieve mental symptoms.

Less serious mental illnesses of the type termed *neuroses* (noo-ROH-seez) may or may not have a cause rooted in biochemistry or genetics, but often the anxieties and fears of neuroses can be reduced with chemical medication.

Recognizing mental illness: Often mental illness is very difficult to diagnose. The patient may want to hide symptoms instead of describing them or may be too confused about reality to be able to differentiate between symptoms of mental illness and ordinary thought. Furthermore, different mental illnesses often have similar symptoms, just as different infectious diseases can produce fever and rash.

Mental illnesses can be grouped in several ways. The complex disease schizophrenia comes closest to the common image of madness. Various forms of depression and mania, including bipolar disorder and clinical depression, are grouped with less severe depressions as *mood disorders;* they, too, can be severe. Ingestion or injection of chemicals can produce many mental symptoms, so alcoholism and drug abuse are treated as mental illnesses as well as physical conditions. Another large group of mental illnesses are the *anxiety disorders;* these include panic attacks and obsessive-compulsive disorder. A group labeled *dissociative disorders* includes both multiple-personality disorder (in which a person changes back and forth from one personality to another) and amnesia. Certain disorders are the result of specific diseases that cause dementia, the medical term for severe confusion and forgetfulness. These include Alzheimer's disease and Creutzfeldt-Jakob disease. *Sexual disorders* range from behaviors that lead to illegal acts, such as sex acts with children, to difficulties in having normal sexual relations.

Some mental disorders are less severe, but still clearly problematic. These include such sleep disorders as insomnia and impulse-control disorders, in which a person cannot control bad habits such as stealing or gambling.

Incidence: Over a lifetime an American has about a 48% chance of developing a condition that might be characterized as mental illness, provided that such conditions as alcoholism and fear of public speaking are included. In a given year about 30% of the population is affected. If the definition of mental disorder is limited to such serious illnesses as various forms of depression, schizophrenia, or multiple-personality disorder, however, the percentage drops dramatically. A study in 2002

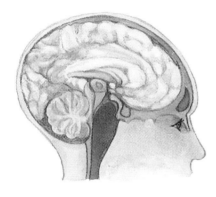

Mental illnesses often involve too much or too little of the neurotransmitters or an incorrect response to them, especially serotonin and dopamine. These chemicals alter moods as they communicate between the cells of the brain.

looked just at those who seek treatment and found 18.5% of Americans are treated each year. The most common serious mental illnesses are clinical depression and alcoholism.

Treatment options: Aside from traditional herbal remedies, confinement was the only treatment for severe mental disorders before modern times. Perhaps the first talking therapy was *hypnosis,* in which a doctor first talks the patient into a receptive state and then either makes suggestions or has the patient describe feelings, or both. In the late nineteenth century hypnosis evolved into psychoanalysis, the most famous talking therapy. In this type of therapy the patient talks to the doctor about dreams and childhood on a regular basis for long periods of time.

Currently, the most popular talking therapies among professionals focus on the patient describing immediate problems while the therapist gives small amounts of advice. In numbers of persons helped, however, the most popular therapy is group self-help, usually modeled on Alcoholics Anonymous (AA). In group self-help people who share a specific problem talk to each other—mostly about the problem but also about their feelings in general. As a treatment method talking therapies have been highly successful with milder neurotic disorders and somewhat less so with addiction disorders.

A different therapy began when some doctors reasoned that disrupting the pathways of the brain might cure incoherent or misdirected thinking. Around 1930 both chemical and electrical shock treatments (known as ECT, for electroconvulsive therapy) were somewhat successful with both schizophrenia and bipolar disorder. The even more profound shock of removing a part of the brain, called prefrontal lobotomy, was also tried. Except for ECT, which is still used for intractable depression, these violent cures have been almost completely abandoned.

Some natural chemicals affect the mind. Tribal healers often used nicotine or chemicals in mushrooms to induce trance states, for example. Artificial chemicals that affect the mind were also discovered, starting with the first barbiturates in 1863. While barbiturates were tried as a treatment for mental illness, they were not very effective. In the 1950s the first minor tranquilizers, such as reserpine, and the major tranquilizers, such as thorazine, were introduced as chemicals to alter moods. In 1964 the U.S. National Institutes of Health found that certain major tranquilizers were effective in treating schizophrenia. Lithium compounds were discovered for the treatment of bipolar disorder; they gradually became popular starting in the early 1970s. Other somewhat effective "psychic energizers" or antidepressants also came into use around that time, and minor tranquilizers combated generalized anxiety and specific phobias. By 1989 more than 36.4 million *new* prescriptions were written for these minor tranquilizers, 81% of them for such drugs as alprazolam (trade name: Xanax) and diazepam (trade name: Valium).

The mid-1980s, however, saw the arrival of a more effective drug for depression too mild to treat with lithium (which can have unpleasant side effects) and too much a part of the personality to disappear easily with talking therapy. Fluoxetine (trade name: Prozac) and similar drugs, called serotonin-uptake inhibitors, elevate *serotonin,* one of the main chemicals used in the brain to signal from one nerve cell to another. For reasons that are poorly understood, higher serotonin levels tend to remove depression and reduce the impulse toward violence in most people. Furthermore, even obsessive-compulsive disorder, previously thought to have no physical basis, often yields to Prozac or other drugs that raise serotonin levels.

Migraine

DISEASE

TYPE: COMBINATION

Migraine has been known as a special kind of headache ever since ancient times. The name comes from a Greek word meaning "half the head," since migraine headaches often occur, or at least begin, on just one side of the head.

A number of features set migraine apart from other kinds of headaches. First of all, migraine headaches are recurrent—they keep coming back, frequently or infrequently. The average is one to three attacks a month, and the attacks tend to be very similar in form. The pain of a migraine headache has a throbbing or knifelike quality, and it can be quite intense and disabling. It may start on just one side of the head and then radiate to the rest of the head or into the neck, shoulders, or back. Attacks may last anywhere from a few hours to several days—a "sunup to sundown" pattern is common.

Among the ways to prevent or reduce the number or severity of migraine headaches is to sit in a comfortable chair with your eyes closed while practicing regular breathing. Try doing this for several minutes every day, keeping the mind either on the breathing process or perhaps visualizing a pleasant scene. More formal methods of meditation can involve special positions and special phrases used to focus attention away from yourself.

The headache is often accompanied by a digestive system upset such as nausea, constipation, or diarrhea. That's why migraine is described as a "sick headache."

The majority of sufferers have *common migraine.* But a minority have *classic migraine.* They not only have recurrent headaches but also experience distinctive sensory disturbances—known collectively as an *aura*—before each attack. Bright spots may appear before the eyes, or parts of the visual field may seem blinded. The visual disturbance may be accompanied by "pins and needles" or other abnormal sensations in the skin. The aura tends to last about half an hour and then disappear. The headache begins shortly afterward.

Cause: Migraine is often described as a *vascular headache.* Vascular headaches originate in the blood vessels (the vascular system), specifically in the arteries that carry blood to the head. Physicians used to think that during an attack the blood vessels swell, stimulating pain-sensing nerves nearby. The throbbing quality of the pain corresponds to the pulse of blood being pumped through the arteries. More modern theories are that the blood vessels become inflamed, perhaps by proteins released by nerves in the brain.

Unlike some other kinds of headaches, migraine seems to be at least partly hereditary. About two of three people who get migraine headaches have near family members who get them too.

In some people migraine attacks are triggered by emotional stress or by drinking or eating particular things, such as alcohol or foods rich in the amino acid *tyramine*. These foods include aged cheese, red wine, and preserved fish. Most migraine attacks, however, are spontaneous—they just happen.

Bright lights, loud noises, strong odors—any strong stimulation of the senses—tend to make the pain worse. Those suffering an attack typically feel a powerful urge to retreat to a dark, quiet place where they can rest until the pain subsides.

Incidence: Migraine is very common, affecting perhaps one person in ten, especially women. About 30% of women between the ages of 21 and 35 are believed to suffer from migraine to some degree, Female hormones may play a part in triggering attacks or making them more severe. Many women have migraine headaches before or during their menstrual periods. Some women find that they do not have attacks during pregnancy. Migraine attacks tend to become less frequent and less severe over time. Many women stop suffering from them about the time they reach menopause.

Noticeable symptoms: Migraine attacks vary among individuals, but they often follow a pattern in a particular individual. They tend to appear about the same time of day and last for about the same length of time. For many sufferers the pain of migraine is distinctive: It throbs at the rate of the pulse.

Diagnosis: There are no special diagnostic tests for migraine. It is generally diagnosed from the symptoms reported by the sufferer.

Treatment options: Migraine attacks can often be controlled by a combination of medications and lifestyle management techniques. Because stress plays a large part in triggering attacks (as it does in other kinds of headaches), relaxation exercises and other stress-management techniques can be very helpful. Another adjustment in lifestyle may be the avoidance of alcohol and foods known to provoke attacks.

Relatively mild migraine headaches may be relieved by common painkillers such as acetaminophen, aspirin, and ibuprofen. A class of drugs called triptans, originating with sumatriptan (trade name: Imitrex) in 1993, acts on the sero-

Rest

No stress

tonin receptors in the brain. The triptans can be very effective, but are not suitable for persons with coronary artery disease.

Prevention: Other drugs may be helpful in preventing migraine attacks as well as making them less severe. Among them are beta blockers and calcium channel blockers, originally used to treat high blood pressure and heart disease. Another drug is methysergide, which is taken between attacks rather than at the beginning of an attack. Some success is also reported with antidepressives such as amitriptyline.

Drugs are not the only preventive measures, however. Regular vigorous exercise helps, probably by increasing the flow of neurotransmitters in the brain.

Exercise

Minamata disease

(MIHN-uh-MAH-tuh)

DISEASE

TYPE: CHEMICAL;
ENVIRONMENTAL

See also
Dementia
Environment and disease
Poisoning

In the mid-1950s fishers and other villagers around Minamata Bay on Kyushu Island, Japan, began to develop neurological problems. There were also many stillbirths and children born with serious defects. Minamata disease gets its name from this outbreak. Eventually, the disease was traced to *mercury poisoning* caused by eating fish from Minamata Bay.

Mercury in lakes and the oceans continues to be a major health concern. Mercury in food remains in the tissue of the consumer. When that consumer is later consumed, as when a big fish eats a smaller fish, the mercury is concentrated at a higher level. Aquatic and marine food chains often stretch through several levels, so mercury in fish tissue can become quite concentrated.

Cause: Mercury is dangerous in all forms, as an element and in all compounds, but it is also extremely useful in industrial processes. The exact mode of mercury poisoning is not clear, but it seems likely that mercury removes sulfur from key proteins, making them useless. It also destroys kidney cells.

The mercury poisoning that affected the Minamata population was caused by industrial wastes that had been dumped in Minamata Bay, polluting the fishing grounds of a people whose main source of protein is fish. All in all, some 17,000 were sickened, and nearly a thousand died.

Because mercury is toxic to all forms of life, it has frequently been used to prevent growth of funguses or other organisms. In 1971 people in Iraq cooked and ate grain intended for seed that had been treated with mercury: 6,530 became ill, and 459 died.

Rain deposits mercury even in remote lakes. Most of the mercury in rainwater comes from air pollution caused by combustion of materials containing mercury. Much of this mercury is released by cement and phosphate plants, while most of the rest comes from incinerators and coal-fired power plants.

Incidence: There are few mass outbreaks like the one at Minamata Bay or in Iraq, but at least 21 U.S. states, 2 Canadian provinces, and Sweden have had to restrict fishing in lakes with high levels of mercury. Typically, pregnant or nursing women and young children are advised not to eat fish from such lakes, while others are told to limit their consumption. The worst lakes for mercury contamination are small, shallow ones, or those newly created by impounding water. Mercury poisoning has been blamed as the source of autism and chronic fatigue syndrome, although evidence is lacking.

Noticeable symptoms: Mercury causes dementia. Mercury fumes are thought to have caused dementia in alchemists or miners who used it to dissolve gold and silver. From the sixteenth to the twentieth century fur used to make felt for hats was treated with nitrate of mercury. Hatters often succumbed to mercury dementia; thus the phrase "as mad as a hatter" entered the language.

Other symptoms include excess saliva, loose teeth and gum disorders, and the appearance of drunkenness. In acute poisoning there may also be bloody diarrhea.

Diagnosis: Severe mercury poisoning leads to kidney failure and death. In slow poisoning there may also be damage to the stomach and intestines.

Treatment options: For acute poisoning one can induce vomiting or try flushing the stomach. Long-term poisoning may be treated with drugs that capture mercury and enable it to be excreted from the body.

Stages and progress: Mercury in water is often converted by bacteria to the compound *methyl mercury*. Methyl mercury is much more easily absorbed by living organisms than elemental mercury. In water it moves up the food chain, where it is concentrated in predator fish. Older, and therefore larger, predator fish are especially prized by humans for food. Methyl mercury also tends to accumulate in the parts of fish that people eat, the muscles. Although levels in fish typically are 10,000 times as high as in the water they live in, fish are not especially affected by methyl mercury poisoning. Humans who eat these fish, especially children, can be harmed.

Miscarriage	*See* **Embryo**

Mitral stenosis and incompetence
(MIY-truhl steh-NOH-sihs)

DISEASE

TYPE: MECHANICAL
(POSSIBLY GENETIC)

See also
Arrhythmias
Atrial fibrillation
Heart
Heart attack
Heart failure
Palpitations
"Strep"

Mitral stenosis and mitral incompetence are separate but similar disorders of the mitral valve of the heart. That valve connects the upper and lower chambers of the left side of the heart. In mitral stenosis the valve is narrower than normal and consequently restricts the passage of blood between the two chambers. This in turn makes the heart work harder to pump blood through the narrowed opening. In mitral incompetence the valve fails to close fully, allowing blood to leak back from one chamber to the other. This forces the heart muscle to work harder to pump the additional load of leaked-back blood through the heart.

Mitral incompetence is also termed *mitral insufficiency* or *mitral regurgitation*. It is also a result of a condition termed *prolapse of the mitral valve*. Some individuals have cases of both mitral stenosis and mitral incompetence at the same time.

Cause: Rheumatic fever, a complication of infection by *Streptococcus* bacteria in childhood or infancy, has been a major cause of both mitral stenosis and mitral incompetence. Scarring of the valve in the course of the fever results in the valve's malfunctioning. However, about half of all those who develop mitral stenosis have no history of rheumatic fever.

Other causes of mitral incompetence include damage to the valve from heart attack or from an incident of heart failure on the heart's left side. An incompetent valve is also thought to be inborn in some cases.

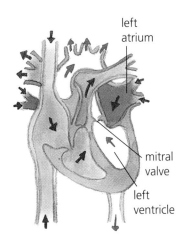

left atrium

mitral valve

left ventricle

Either narrowing of the mitral valve (stenosis) or failure of the valve to work properly (incompetence) eventually produces damage to heart muscle.

Incidence: Perhaps one person in ten has mitral valve problems, but usually with no harm to health.

Noticeable symptoms: Shortness of breath during exertion is one of the first signs of mitral stenosis. Breathing difficulty typically increases and eventually appears after very little exertion or even while sitting or lying down. In advanced cases symptoms can include irregular heartbeats (called palpitations or fibrillation), signs of heart failure (flushed cheeks, bluish lips, and ankle swelling), and coughing attacks that bring up bloodstained mucus.

Mitral incompetence is also evidenced by shortness of breath and weakness, but these are often less pronounced than in mitral stenosis.

Diagnosis: Cardiologists recognize the typical heart murmur from its sound as heard through a stethoscope. An echocardiogram, which checks both electrical activity and movement of blood in the heart, is used to confirm diagnosis.

Treatment: Beta blockers to control blood pressure and heart rate, diuretics to reduce swelling, or digitalis compounds to counter heart failure are often prescribed. If stenosis is causing atrial fibrillation, drugs to prevent clot formation may be prescribed. Heart surgery to repair a defective valve or to replace it with an artificial one can remedy the conditions in severe cases.

Because bacteria that further damage valves can move into the heart after dental work or surgery, antibiotics should be taken prior to any procedure that causes bleeding.

Moles and freckles

DISEASE

TYPE: UNKNOWN; GENETIC; CANCER

Moles—also called *nevi* (NEE-viy), singular *nevus*—are small, light-to-dark-colored growths on the skin. They are almost always clusters of pigment cells among other skin cells. Nearly everyone has at least some, but people with fair skin tend to have them in greater numbers. Freckles—small, flat brown spots—are a common discoloration of the skin caused by exposure to the sun.

Most moles are round, have a clearly defined symmetrical shape, and are smaller than three-sixteenth of an inch. They may be flat or raised, with color ranges from flesh tones to dark brown or black. Moles rarely pose health problems, but the

Phone doctor

serious skin cancer melanoma sometimes starts in a mole. *Changes in size, color, or shape of a mole may be a sign that a cancer is developing and should be checked by your doctor as soon as possible.*

Cause: Common moles are clusters of skin pigment cells that begin growing at the point where the outer layer of the skin meets the layer underneath it.

Freckles have a different origin. Heredity figures in the tendency to form them, but freckles themselves initially appear in response to sunlight. As a result freckles are an indication of the possible development of skin cancer, also caused by the sun.

Incidence: Eventually about 95% of all people develop at least a few moles, and about 1% of people of European descent are born with them. An estimated 5 to 10% of Americans have one or more moles that are what doctors call "atypical." These moles are unusually large and irregularly shaped or show other signs that they could become cancerous.

Noticeable symptoms: Moles, either raised or flat, that are symmetrical in shape and do not change in size or color usually are no cause for concern, even if there are many of them. But if a mole is growing, becomes irregular in shape, has a mixture of brown, black, or other colors, itches, bleeds, or becomes inflamed or painful, then melanoma may be a possibility. *See a doctor as soon as possible if any of these symptoms develop.* Early detection of melanoma dramatically improves the chances of curing it.

A doctor should also look at any freckles or liver spots that are irregular in shape or uneven in color, or that exhibit the symptoms mentioned above.

Diagnosis: Generally, if your doctor is suspicious about an atypical mole, he or she will remove it and have it analyzed to see if cancer cells are present.

Treatment options: Large or atypical moles can be removed surgically, usually in the doctor's office. Giant moles may have to be removed in stages, however, because of their size.

Prevention: Generally, you cannot prevent moles from growing in the first place, but you should take care to avoid irritat-

Phone doctor

See also
Melanoma
Skin
Skin cancers
Skin diseases
Warts

Port wine stains and liver spots

Babies are sometimes born with a skin discoloration called, from its reddish purple color, a port wine stain (also called *nevus flammeus*). In some cases the discoloration may cover an area larger than the child's open hand. The skin's pigment cells are not involved in this skin discoloration. Instead, an abnormal cluster of capillaries darkens the skin. Port wine stains are not physically harmful, although if near the eyes they may predispose a person to glaucoma. If a port wine stain is disfiguring, it may be removed surgically with a yellow laser while the child is an infant.

Skin discolorations called liver spots (or *solar lentigo*) can appear on people over age 40 as a result of a lifetime of exposure to sunlight. These are typically brown or beige and may be as big as a dime. Liver spots can usually be faded or cleared up completely with regular applications for six to ten months of a medication called tretinoin, by chemical peeling, laser surgery, or cryosurgery.

ing them whenever possible. Where clothing regularly rubs against a mole, having it removed might be a good idea, especially if it has become inflamed or swollen. Children who use sunscreen regularly develop fewer new moles or freckles.

Mononucleosis

(MON-oh-noo-klee-OH-sihs)

DISEASE

TYPE: INFECTIOUS (VIRAL)

Young adults between 15 and 30 are more likely than others to get mononucleosis. If someone feels ill and extremely tired for several days in a row, mononucleosis may be the cause.

Cause: Mononucleosis, also called *infectious mononucleosis,* is a contagious disease caused by the Epstein-Barr virus (EBV), a type of herpesvirus. The disease is spread by contact, usually contact with the saliva of an infected person.

Incidence: In the United States mononucleosis is most common among young adults of college age. Because it is contagious through infected droplets of saliva, it can be transmitted through kissing and thus is sometimes known as *kissing disease.* In less developed parts of world mononucleosis occurs in children as young as two years of age. It is not uncommon for siblings to pass it on to one another. Rarely, mononucleosis occurs as a result of receiving a blood transfusion.

Noticeable symptoms: In young children the disease is mild and may go unnoticed. An older child may have a mild sore throat or tonsillitis. Symptoms in young adults are more severe. They may include headache, swollen eyelids, chills, severe fatigue, and loss of appetite. Patients may also run a fever, have a sore throat for several days, and experience swollen glands in the neck, underarms, or groin area for several weeks. There may be difficulty in swallowing, bleeding gums, skin rash, or bruising. A rarer symptom is jaundice, which indicates a problem with liver function.

Diagnosis: Because mononucleosis has some symptoms similar to those of "strep" throat, meningitis, rubella ("German" measles), appendicitis, and even some forms of cancer, it is important to see a physician to get a diagnosis. A physical examination may reveal swollen lymph nodes or an enlarged spleen, which occurs in 50% of cases, or an enlarged liver, which occurs in 20%.

By examining a blood sample, a physician can see if an abnormally large number of *mononuclear white blood cells,* called lymphocytes or monocytes, are circulating through the bloodstream (this is how the disease gets its name). Since these are the main cells that fight bacteria and viruses, a large number of them suggests that the immune system is hard at work.

Treatment options: Treating mononucleosis has changed somewhat in recent years as physicians have learned more about the virus that causes it. In the past bed rest for four to six weeks and limited activity for several months were recommended. Today, however, physicians prescribe a shorter bed rest period, from six to ten days, and anticipate full recovery in four to six weeks. However, doctors recommend avoiding strenuous exercise to prevent damage to the spleen if it has become enlarged with the infection.

Home care includes relief of symptoms such as gargling with saltwater to soothe a sore throat. Fluids to prevent dehydration and a nutritious diet are also important. To relieve pain, over-the-counter pain relievers such as acetaminophen (for example, Tylenol) can be taken. However, *children and teenagers should not take aspirin because of the risk of Reye's syndrome,* a potentially harmful condition of the nervous system and liver.

Antibiotics do not affect the Epstein-Barr virus or any other virus. However, about a third of the people with mononucleosis also develop "strep" throat, and antibiotics are used against the

Gargle saltwater   Drink water

Avoid aspirin

streptococcus bacteria that causes it. Some antibiotics must be avoided, however, as they almost always provoke an outbreak of an itchy rash.

Stages and progress: Symptoms of mononucleosis may appear four to six weeks after exposure to the Epstein-Barr virus, and progress varies from person to person. The greatest danger of going without treatment is a ruptured spleen. Most people recover fully from mononucleosis without complications.

Prevention: Avoid close contact with a person who has mononucleosis. Keep immunity up by getting enough rest. If you do get the disease, it imparts immunity for life.

Motion sickness

DISEASE

TYPE: MECHANICAL

See also
Balance
Dizziness
Headache
Nausea
Seasickness
Senses

Traveling by car, train, airplane, or boat sometimes causes motion sickness, an unpleasant feeling of dizziness accompanied by headache, nausea, and in more severe cases, vomiting. Anyone can suffer motion sickness if the conditions are right, such as a bumpy airplane flight in stormy weather, especially if the passenger has eaten or drunk too much. Some people are more sensitive to the effects of motion than others, and even the relatively gentle movement felt during a routine flight or car trip can trigger a bout of motion sickness. In almost all cases the discomfort disappears with no lasting effects once the trip is over.

Cause: Motion sickness begins in the inner ear. Each ear contains three fluid-filled semicircular canals and tiny organs called the utricle and saccule; these combine to sense balance. Vertical motion, such as that experienced on a bumpy plane flight or even during a ride in an elevator, can stimulate these organs into a feeling of falling that can lead to dizziness, nausea, and vomiting. Other factors also enter in, however. The different signals that reach the brain from the eyes and from the balance organs in the ear can be part of the problem. For some persons the brain reacts to such conflicting signals with motion sickness. One does not even need to be moving: Some 30% of those who use advanced virtual reality equipment are affected by motion sickness. This is probably because of the difference between visual and balance-organ messages to the brain.

Other forms of motion sickness are harder to understand. Some persons, for example, experience motion sickness if they stare at a fixed object in a vehicle; thus they cannot read while riding in a car or train. The smoother motion and more complete enclosure of an airplane, however, may produce no motion sickness while reading in flight.

Incidence: While only a small fraction of people who travel by car, train, or air suffer motion sickness, the problem is not uncommon.

Noticeable symptoms: A mild case of motion sickness may involve nothing more than dizziness, headache, sweating, and a queasy feeling in the stomach. Severe motion sickness can be quite debilitating though. People may vomit uncontrollably and be unable to keep fluids or foods down. They may turn pale, have cold and clammy skin, and, weakened by vomiting and dizziness, find it hard to remain standing or even sitting upright.

Treatment options: If medication is needed, a doctor may recommend sedatives or antihistamines such as dimenhydrinate (Dramamine), promethazine, or meclizine for use before and during a trip. Scopolamine is available by prescription in patch form.

Prevention: For severe or persistent motion sickness the best approach is to take preventive medicine before traveling.

Some forms of motion sickness can be prevented or alleviated by gazing at the vehicle in which you are riding; for example, looking at the floor or interior of a car instead of at the apparent motion of objects outside the car.

Space sickness

Some of the most severe motion sickness occurs in space capsules that orbit Earth, including U.S. space shuttles. It is not the great speed of about 20,000 mph that causes this form of motion sickness, called space sickness. People in an orbiting satellite are in free fall, also known as weightlessness. Every part of the spaceship is falling toward Earth as it also speeds forward. The result is that the fluids in the inner ear and small stones called otoliths in the utricle and saccule act as if gravity no longer exists. With no apparent up or down the whole sense of balance is disrupted, and motion sickness can be severe. At first space travelers may feel intense nausea. After a while the brain retrains itself to ignore the signals of falling that are coming from the inner ear. The orbiting traveler's space sickness ends. But there will be another period of adjustment to come when the traveler returns to Earth.

Mountain sickness   *See* **Polycythemia**

Multiple myeloma
(MIY-uh-LOH-muh)

DISEASE

TYPE: CANCER

See also
Back and spine problems
Bone diseases
Cancers
Immune system
Leukemia
Lymphocytes
Lymphoma
Phagocytes and other leukocytes

Multiple myeloma (also called *Kahler's disease* or *myelomatosis*) is a cancer of certain white blood cells found in bone marrow and in connective tissue. These cells, known as *plasma cells*, are formed in the red marrow as are some other types of white blood cells. Plasma cells, which are fewer in number than the more familiar cells that circulate in the blood and lymph, ordinarily function as part of the body's immune system, creating antibodies against infection. Although they are technically white blood cells, few are found in the blood. They are closely related to the B lymphocytes (see Lymphocytes).

Cause: The cause of abnormal reproduction of plasma cells is unknown. When plasma cells reproduce in abnormal numbers and forms to produce multiple myeloma, they interfere with the production of red blood cells, causing anemia, and of platelets, impairing blood clotting. The cells' main harm, however, comes from producing very large amounts of an immune protein that injures nearby bones, especially the flat bones such as ribs, eroding them and making them susceptible to fracture. Finally, the abnormal cells do not produce normal antibodies, so that the body's immune system is weakened.

Incidence: Multiple myeloma is relatively rare, occurring in 1 in 25,000 people, accounting for nearly 13,000 deaths a year in the United States.

It is twice as common in men as in women and twice as common in African Americans as in European Americans. It occurs nearly always among people over 40, with most who develop the disease in their seventies or older.

Noticeable symptoms: The most common symptom is pain in the bones, particularly those in the back. Sometimes the bones of the upper and lower jaws are attacked, causing teeth to loosen. Fatigue and breathlessness typical of anemia are also possible, as are nosebleeds or bleeding gums. General resistance to infection is lowered.

Diagnosis: The first sign of the disease is often anemia revealed in a routine blood test. Multiple myeloma is further diagnosed with the help of blood tests and x-rays. A common condition caused by the disease is thinning of bones, which releases calcium into the bloodstream.

Drink water

Treatment options: Drinking a lot of water is recommended—it helps keep the blood fluid and thus protects the kidneys from damage by excess calcium or antibodies—along with regular but mild exercise to help build up bone mass.

The bone pain is treated with painkillers ranging from aspirin to opiates. Antibiotics may be given to help replace lost immune functions, and steroids to reduce inflammation.

The disease is often found in blood tests long before symptoms occur. After symptoms begin to occur, the production of abnormal plasma cells is attacked with the same methods used for other forms of cancer—chemotherapy (anticancer drugs) and radiation. These techniques are potentially harmful to all cells, but they are most destructive to cells that reproduce especially fast, such as cancer cells. Occasionally, bone marrow transplantation is helpful.

The progress of the disease can be slowed by treatment, but it is eventually fatal, often as a result of infection or bleeding. Five-year survival rates have quadrupled, however, since the 1950s—more than a quarter of all patients, most of whom are quite elderly, survive for five or more years.

Multiple-personality syndrome

DISEASE

TYPE: MENTAL

See also
Mental illnesses

A patient with multiple-personality syndrome, more properly called *dissociative identity disorder,* has two or more identities that behave and react differently from each other. Each separate set of responses, temperaments, and often memories is called a *personality, identity,* or *alter* (for alter-ego). People with over 100 distinct personalities have been reported. Usually, one personality, called the *primary,* is dominant much of the time, but any one of the other *secondary* personalities is capable of taking over.

Cause: Physical abuse, sexual abuse, or other severe emotional or physical trauma during childhood can heighten normal internal conflicts and lead to dissociative identity disorder. Physical or sexual abuse from a parent or other family member, for example, can arouse intense feelings of fear and anxiety in a child. Coping with those emotions can be extremely difficult, and avoiding the emotional conflict altogether may seem to be the only alternative. Multiple-personality patients cope, experts think, by separating conflicting emotions into different personalities.

Incidence: Once thought to be extremely rare, dissociative identity disorder has been diagnosed more frequently in the United States in the last 50 years. One estimate is that as many as 1 in 40 of all hospitalized psychiatric patients have this disorder; this does not account for the large number of persons treated as outpatients. A complication is that the various alters can themselves exhibit mental illnesses, especially depression but sometimes schizophrenia.

Women suffer this illness more often than men.

Noticeable symptoms: All of us at one time or another do things that seem completely out of character. But with the person suffering dissociative identity disorder, the change from one set of behaviors to another is surprisingly complete and at times even the exact opposite of the person's normal responses. Secondary personalities of multiple-personality patients may adopt different styles of clothing, different habits such as smoking or drinking alcohol, and different ways of speaking, as well as a host of changed personality traits.

The most serious consequence of dissociative identity disorder is suicide, which is much more common for this syndrome than for other mental illnesses.

Treatment options: Therapists use hypnosis and psychotherapy to help make the primary personality aware of the secondary personality. At the same time, the patient is taught that having conflicting needs and wants is part of being human, and that too much self-criticism can be harmful. Treatment may take several years and is not always successful.

Multiple sclerosis

(skluh-ROH-sihs)

DISEASE

TYPE: AUTOIMMUNE

See also
ALS (amyotrophic lateral sclerosis)
Autoimmune diseases
Nerves
Nervous system
Viruses and disease

Multiple sclerosis (MS) is a serious disease that affects nerves in various parts of the body. The muscles are indirectly affected because they no longer receive accurate messages through the nervous system.

Cause: Doctors do not know exactly what causes MS, but they have learned that an immune response to a virus starts it. The viral disease does not damage nerves directly. The patient's immune system does that by its response to the virus. People who develop MS seem to have an inherited immune response to the virus. Their bodies mistakenly produce antibodies that attack the nerve's insulating sheath, which is made from a white, fatty tissue called *myelin* (MIY-uh-lihn). Without the myelin insulation messages fail to travel along the nerves.

During an attack the antibodies cause the myelin sheath to swell and become inflamed, producing a patch called a *sclerosis*. The name of the disease comes from the presence of many such patches. Repeated attacks can destroy parts of the myelin completely.

MS is more common in temperate zones than in the tropics and subtropics. Reduced levels of vitamin D among those living in more northerly regions might be a factor (when days are short, people are exposed to less sunlight, needed to produce vitamin D).

There is also a genetic form of multiple sclerosis that causes about 2 to 3% of all incidences of the disease. The symptoms are the same, but the cause is probably different.

Incidence: MS occurs in about one out of every thousand persons. Women are 50% more likely to get the disease than men. People of European descent are five times as likely to develop the disease as those of African descent. The actual extent of MS is difficult to estimate, however, because mild cases may not even be reported to doctors and may be misdiagnosed when they are. One estimate is that 200,000 Americans have the disease.

Usually MS patients suffer their first attack between the ages of 20 and 40.

Noticeable symptoms: The disease usually begins with tingling, numbness, or weakness in an arm or leg, or in one spot somewhere else on the body. If an arm is affected, the victim may drop items more often than normal because the muscles are unexpectedly weak. If it is a leg, the victim may sometimes drag a foot. Other parts of the body may be affected as well. There may be fatigue and temporarily blurred or double vision, unsteady movement, slurring of words, and difficulty with urination. Sometimes there are mental problems such as confusion or poor memory, a mild dementia.

Phone doctor

Whatever symptoms occur, they almost always clear up without treatment after a few days or weeks. *Any one of these symptoms is serious enough to warrant medical attention, however, and a doctor should be seen as soon as possible.*

Diagnosis: MS is capable of producing a wide range of symptoms depending on which nerves have become inflamed. This makes diagnosis of the disease difficult, for other neurological disorders may also cause some of the same symptoms. For those reasons a diagnosis of MS is usually based on extensive tests as well as the patient's past history of attacks and remissions.

An EEG (electroencephalogram) or MRI (magnetic resonance imaging) scan may help pinpoint areas of damage to nerves, and blood tests may help doctors eliminate other possible disorders, such as vitamin deficiencies and vascular inflammations, that could cause similar symptoms. A sample of the patient's cerebrospinal fluid (a spinal tap) will probably also be tested for a telltale protein in the fluid that is caused by an inflammatory reaction in the central nervous system.

Treatment options: The drug beta interferon (common trade names are Betaseron, Avonex, and Rebif) has been shown to slow the course of MS. Beta interferon modulates a response involved in the immune attack on the myelin sheath. One other drug, glatiramer acetate (trade name: Copaxone), is also known to be helpful. New drugs are being developed.

There can also be symptomatic relief. When patients have trouble talking or walking during an attack, corticosteroid drugs or corticotrophin helps control these symptoms. Doctors may also prescribe medication to control problems with spastic muscle movement and with bladder control.

Stages and progress: Usually, the disease begins with an outbreak of mild symptoms such as numbness or weakness in an arm or leg. These early symptoms almost always clear up by themselves, and some people do not experience worsening.

For some, however, the episodes continue, appearing sporadically months or even years apart. Between attacks the MS goes into remission (the symptoms disappear), but eventually the chronic flareups cause permanent, disabling nerve damage. Depending on the severity of their attacks, MS sufferers may continue to lead relatively normal lives for up to 20 or 30 years after the disease first appears.

For those patients with the pattern of recurring MS and remission recovery may be almost complete after each of the early episodes. But over time repeated attacks cause cumulative damage to the patient's nerves, resulting in less complete recovery and finally permanent nerve damage. Although it may take many years, MS patients eventually suffer progressive weakness of the arms and legs, loss of vision, and other problems.

In the rare and most severe form of MS the disease progresses steadily after it first appears and does not go into remission. Thus permanent nerve damage and serious disability occur much sooner.

Outlook: About 70% of those diagnosed with MS continue to live relatively normal lives five years or more after diagnosis. Most persons with MS must make adjustments in the way they live, however. They can help prevent new episodes of disease symptoms by following an exercise and diet regimen designed for general good health. It helps to avoid overexertion, emotional stress, extremes of heat and cold, and sources of infection. In this way most people with MS continue to lead productive lives for many years. Studies have reported potential benefits from regular intake of vitamin D supplements.

Exercise

No stress

INDEX

Our thanks to the following organizations and persons who
made the photographs used in this set possible:

Christ Episcopal Church Youth Program (Mary Millan)
Mount Vernon Teen Task Force (Chris Webb)
Putnam Family Support and Advocacy, Inc. (Pam Forde)

Photography assistant: Tania Gandy-Collins

MODELS

Roland Benson, Sally Bunch, Deirdre Burke, Kevin Chapin,
Michael Clarke, Michelle Collins, Bryan Duggan, Germaine
Elvy, Caitlin Faughnan, Imgard Kallenbach, Max Lipson, Lydia
McCarthy, Amanda Moradel, Joshua Moradel, Veronica
Moradel, Kate Peckham, Sara Pettinger, Mario Salinas,
Heather Scogna, Halima Simmons, Wendy Sinclair, T.J.
Trancynger, Rolando Walker, Deborah Whelan, Gregory
Whelan, Francis Wick, Elaine Young, Leanne Young